Terrorism

Trauma

and **Tragedies:**

A Counselor's Guide to Preparing and Responding

edited by DEBRA D. BASS
AND RICHARD YEP

American Counseling Association Foundation
Alexandria, Virginia

Terrorism, Trauma, and Tragedies: A Counselor's Guide to Preparing and Responding
© 2002 by the American Counseling Association Foundation
5999 Stevenson Avenue
Alexandria, VA 22304

All rights reserved.
Printed in the United States of America.

American Counseling Association Foundation
5999 Stevenson Avenue
Alexandria, VA 22304

10   9   8   7   6   5   4   3   2

Cover design by Martha Woolsey

Library of Congress Cataloging-in-Publication Data

Terrorism, trauma and tragedies: a counselor's guide to preparing and responding/edited by Debra D. Bass and Richard Yep.

p.cm.

ISBN 1-55620-225-3
1. September 11 Terrorist Attacks, 2001—Psychological aspects. 2. Terrorism—United States—Psychological aspects. 3. Victims of terrorism—Counseling of—United States. 4. Crisis intervention (Mental health services)—United States. I. Bass, Debra D. II. Yep, Richard, 1956-

HV6432.T472 2002
362.2'04251—dc21   2002074578

This book is dedicated to all who work with children, adolescents and young adults. The world as we would like to see it really is in your hands.

CONTENTS

Every book begins with an idea, a thought, or a commitment to communicate something that will be of interest or importance to the reader. This publication, *Terrorism, Trauma and Tragedies: A Counselor's Guide to Preparing and Responding*, is no exception.

Conceived as a resource for counselors, teachers, administrators, parents and others, this is a hands-on, practical book that provides useful information and guidance on strategies, techniques and plans that have worked well. It was not developed as a theoretical or formal text on the root causes of terrorism or tragedy, so much as something that caregivers can pick up and use immediately in their practice with children, adolescents, teens, and adults of all ages who are experiencing the trauma of a tragic event.

This book is a collection of original material, news stories, handouts, and even adaptations of recent conference presentations. As such, it includes a variety of writing styles and approaches. In Section 1, for example, you will read straight-from-the-heart, moving, personal accounts of counselors who were on the front lines on September 11th and afterward. It is important to hear their stories in their own words.

The Trustees of the American Counseling Association Foundation formulated the idea for this publication shortly after the terrorist attacks. While they had contemplated some type of resource in the wake of school shootings and other tragedies over the past few years, the events of September 11th dictated that the book move into an accelerated production schedule. This is the first book published by the Foundation.

It is the hope of the ACA Foundation that this book will be a resource to helping professionals as they grapple with how best to work with persons who are facing tragic and traumatic events in their lives, indeed in today's world. Terrorism has become a fact of life in recent months. As Jill Riethmayer notes in Chapter 25, things will never be the same again in our country and in the world, and we all must conceive a new "normal." This book is a first step in that endeavor.

We look forward to your thoughts and comments on the usefulness of this resource. We would especially appreciate your suggestions on improvements for future editions. Please contact us via e-mail at ACAF@counseling.org, or via phone at 1-800-347-6647, ext. 231.

The American Counseling Association Foundation (2001–2002)

Jane Webber Runte, Chair
William Cox, Immediate Past Chair
Quincy Moore, Chair-Elect
James Henderson, Trustee
Clemmie Solomon, Trustee-Designate
Jane Goodman, ACA President
David Kaplan, ACA President-Elect
Richard Yep, Secretary-Treasurer

ACKNOWLEDGMENT

The Trustees of the ACA Foundation wish to thank the many authors and organizations that contributed material to this book. Our heartfelt appreciation for your fine work. The editors especially want to thank ACA Foundation Chair, Jane Webber Runte, who issued a clarion call to many of her colleagues in New York and New Jersey urging them to share their September 11th experiences for the benefit of the profession.

Last, but certainly not least, we want to thank the helping professionals for whom this book was both produced and dedicated. The good work that you do everyday for millions of individuals is something that continues to drive the ACA Foundation to develop projects such as this one. You are extraordinary in what you do and we hope that our efforts will be of use to you in your professional endeavors.

We also thank the organizations listed below for generously allowing us to include their material.

Contributing Organizations

American Association of Pastoral Counselors
CDC Public Response Service
ERIC Counseling and Student Services Clearinghouse
Electronic Recruiting Exchange
National Association of School Psychologists
National Institute of Mental Health
National Mental Health Association
Texas Counseling Association

Section One

Personal Reflections on September 11th, 2001

Personal Reflections on September 11th, 2001 ...from Roxbury High School, New Jersey

Jane Webber Runte

1

Few high school events are life changing. Students worry about junior prom dates, passing their driver's license, or getting into college. As I look back on my own high school years, I vividly remember a few life-changing days: the day JFK was shot—I was a high school freshman at an U.S. Army Band concert; the day students died at Kent State—I was a college student, shocked and vulnerable; the day Martin Luther King was assassinated—I lost my hero; the day after the massacre at the Munich Olympics, I stayed to honor the athletes. I was more than an American living abroad—I was part of the world community in mourning and shock.

September 11th dramatically changed all our lives—students, teachers, families, and counselors. That Tuesday was a day of disbelief, shock, wrenching fear, and grief. The first reports of the attacks came from colleagues hearing it on CNN. Word spread quickly among the seven schools and 5,000 students and staff. Solemnly, the crisis team prepared a message and moved to respond. We walked from room to room, quietly alerting teachers of their role.

Students streamed into the counseling center to connect, to talk, and to cry. Most came quietly, some were sobbing, some were panic-sticken. The counseling center was subdued and supportive. TVs were turned off. Most students anxiously sought to call parents in the World Trade Center (WTC). Not connecting with a parent was unbelievably troubling. Lines were jammed and constantly busy. After getting busy signals, counselors helped them step aside to let the next student call.

That morning it was vital to connect with parents and hear their voices. Tears of relief flowed when a parent answered the phone. Students hugged each other and cried. We helped them find their brothers or sisters in other schools to reassure them. Relatives phoned in messages. Amazingly, a phone call came

through from a school counselor in Kentucky. She received a call from a dad who escaped and was huddled on a ferry with his coworkers. This counselor was the only person he could reach. She gave us several names and phone numbers so we could inform others of the dads' safety and continue the chain. Connecting with loved ones brought relief and reassurance.

Miracle stories spread throughout the building. A parent missed his regular train by seconds to take a call from his daughter—he would have been at work on the 95th floor. One dad took a later train because his son overslept—he said he'd never complain about being late again. Another parent was on the train coming in to the WTC when it suddenly stopped and was diverted.

One dad told his son not to worry. He was told to go back to his classroom, and then the line went dead. His son tried to call again and again without success. Counselors and friends took the freshman, his mother, and family home and began a vigil. We all prayed silently for his dad's safety. When my phone rang at 4:30 a.m. I knew his dad had arrived home.

The immediate safety of our students was paramount. Teachers and custodians walked the halls to keep our building calm, scooping up distressed students from classes. Members of the clergy joined us quickly. We calmed panicked students, united them with siblings, and remained by their side for support. Teachers found extra chairs, cell phones, bottled water, and cookies. They walked the halls with students needing to cool down, and brought back more students who needed assistance. The school became a caring community. Students met younger siblings in the elementary schools. We checked emergency cards for parents who worked in New York City and at the WTC, making sure someone would be at home before students got on the buses.

Parents rushed to the building to take their children home. Although anxious neighbors wanted to

3

pick students up, we needed permission from parents to release them. It was difficult to explain this to distressed friends and relatives, but they soon appreciated our concern. We tried to assess parents and students when they arrived and before they left, but this became a super-human task. Some parents were so distressed that we kept them in the center until we reached a friend or relative. We called neighbors to take parents home who were too upset to drive.

Many teachers and support staff had family members who were at the WTC or who were rescue workers at Ground Zero. Other teachers volunteered to substitute so that they could make phone calls, speak with a counselor, or cry privately. Slowly, through the day and evening, children, husbands, wives and parents were accounted for. I faced my own fears for a few brief moments when I tried unsuccessfully to connect with my daughter at GWU, a few blocks from the White House. I worried about my niece, nephew and brother-in-law who were working in Manhattan. I had to go on automatic pilot or my worst fears would consume me.

The parents of our school children came home. Some arrived late or the next day, but they all came home. In my town of Bernardsville and neighboring Basking Ridge, closer to the city, many were unaccounted for. Counselors and clergy walked commuter parking lots with family members, praying that their loved one's car was NOT left in the lot. A car still there was a symbol that dad or mom was not coming home. Meeting the trains that day and evening was surrealistic—ash covered ghosts silently descended the steps to return to the living. Families stood at attention, armed with cell phones trying to find their loved one among the specters of humanity.

Survivors and their families needed our immediate support and counseling. They were both joyous and sad—guilt ridden that they had survived and friends had not. Others were glued to the TV looking for a clue, a face. Many students were uncertain how to respond. They spoke in hushed tones and the building's silence was disarming. They were angry, sad, and confused. They felt vulnerable. Students worried if it was all right to feel relieved that they were spared from the tragedy.

Parents agonized over what to say to their children. They wanted answers that made it less painful. We shared questions and suggested responses to them, borrowing resources from organizations such as ACA and ASCA. Often we were stymied as well. There were no good answers for students, just ways to try to soothe the anguish. We decided to go on with our Freshman Parent Guidance Night as an opportunity for parents

to come together. Many worried about the impact of the WTC after the deaths of two popular students in a car wreck last winter and the death of a baby in a house fire nearby. Death was too close to talk about it.

Students came to hang out early in the morning or late in the afternoon after sports. They needed "down" time and did not want to be pushed to talk. Some found the school routine a welcome relief from nonstop TV news coverage at home. Others had difficulty concentrating in class. Many students were scared to share their feelings openly. Others were angry with everyone—teachers, parents, and the world.

Students wanted to do something—anything. They needed to respond and to offer help. They were uncomfortable doing nothing. We brought student groups together and they planned a memorial assembly, a peace wall in the cafeteria, and a peace pole project. One student volunteered to sing God Bless America before the football games. Others adopted a firehouse in New York City. Students donated blood. Clubs made patriotic pins. A senior created a riveting film memorial. The student assembly mobilized more than 100 students. Students from Africa and South America spoke from their hearts about racism, hatred, and intolerance, and also the hope of acceptance and peace. When an RHS grad, a firefighter at Ground Zero, shared his experiences and showed his photos of the first days, the auditorium was solemn and hushed.

Slowly life started to return to a routine. We had to begin again. When we finally heard the jets overhead circling Newark Airport, the silence was broken. Bravely and still cautiously, we went to Yankee games, played football and soccer, and attended memorials, vigils, and funerals.

Last year we helped students learn the rituals of a wake and paying respects to the students who died. This year there were funerals without bodies, rituals without burials. Each day we read obituaries, lists of missing persons, stories of heroism, and pleas for help to find loved ones. In my own neighborhood, funerals were scheduled, two each day, day after day. Death was all around us. Yet in the midst of grief, babies were born to widows, and communities rallied to help families go on living.

Everyone felt vulnerable and continued to talk about safety. Anthrax and terrorism on American soil were troubling new threats. Just as families struggled to get back into the college process, applications and transcripts were lost when New Jersey Post Offices and distribution centers were closed. Colleges were understanding and flexible, and we survived by fax and e-mail.

Seniors looked back on a difficult and tragic year. Some found it hard to look to the future and make plans to move on. Decisions were made more slowly. Students thought about enlisting to serve their country. Families talked about college differently: How close is it to home? How easy is it to get home? Is it safe? Some seniors needed more time before moving on. Time was a special gift to give this year—students needed time to make sense of all that happened to them.

Students were more cautious and more caring. They drove more carefully, checked in with parents and grandparents often, and tried to make each day count. One senior started to say good night to her dad every evening because he leaves for Manhattan before she rises in the morning. Family Nights at school were well attended. Students looked out for each other and they often brought their friends to talk with their counselors. Volunteering and acts of kindness were up. Students and teachers solemnly recited the Pledge of Allegiance in the morning—slowly with more emphasis and more attention. The Veterans Day Assembly had greater meaning for all of us.

As we approached the holidays, we struggled with being festive while we grieved. Red and white poinsettias took their traditional place on our desks. We were a little late gift-wrapping our doors, and the building was very subdued. Students looked for predictability, security, and direction. How could they try to celebrate and not feel guilty? How could they take the train and not imagine those who died in the empty seats around them? In December, my couch was often crowded with wistful, weeping students.

With the New Year, everyone wished for a return to normal. They slowly realized that after this unspeakable tragedy, life could never be the way it used to be. The change was forever. With winter, the student silence returned—a scary silence. One day, the huge murals of athletes that lined the cafeteria walls were gone. In its place on the wall, penned by students, was this:

September 11, 2001

Tragic, Unthinkable

Shocking, Mind-numbing, Heart-Breaking

Terrorism, Chaos, Unity, Hope

Rebuilding, Remembering, Healing

Strong, Determined

Triumph

Their lives, though brutally changed, found a future. Through the hurt and grief, the agonizing uncertainty, and sad farewells, students began to feel that life went on. We had helped them grope through the darkness. Nothing in grad school ever prepared us for this.

Jane Webber Runte, LPC, Chairperson of the ACA Foundation (2001-02), is also Assistant Principal for Guidance/Related Services at Roxbury High School.

...FROM PIER 94, NEAR GROUND ZERO, NEW YORK CITY

Samuel T. Gladding

Literally thousands of words have been written about the tragedy of the September 11th terrorists' attack on the World Trade Centers (WTC). The incident stunned us and still seems incomprehensible. We watched much of it on television yet even now we still have a hard time believing our eyes, even when we see replays. The magnitude of the event and the sheer number of people killed and injured were so great as to seem at first glance fictitious. However, with each passing day, news accounts reveal to us in graphic and personal details the reality of the incident. All of us were involved as participants in some way as we witnessed then and relive in our minds now, a morning of horror that left us in shock, sorrow, and sadness. The world changed and became more unsafe and unstable in the senseless sacrifice of innocent people.

In response to what we witnessed and felt, many of us wanted to do something constructive. We were able to in a number of ways, for in the immediate aftermath the situation required a multitude of services. Thus, we joined together in making donations to the families of the victims, giving blood to support the hospitals and Red Cross workers who were attending the wounded, and writing letters to support the rescue workers as well as to console those who had lost loved ones. There were teach-ins that we participated in, too, so that information concerning the Middle East and Muslim faith was more accurately understood. These activities were therapeutic both for us as givers as well as for those who were the recipients of our efforts.

Another chance to serve in the hard hit areas of Washington and New York came in the form of volunteer service. Thus, when I was asked to go to New York to work as a "mental health technician" for the American Red Cross, I did not hesitate. It was an opportunity that I realized would not come again and that was important to answer positively. Thanks to the

National Board for Certified Counselors (NBCC), I was able to get my credentials together quickly and to arrange for an almost immediate flight.

Starting on the 15th day after the attack, the day the emphasis of the search at the WTC went from rescue to recovery, I worked for a week as a counselor. My assigned site was in the Family Assistance Center on Pier 94, where families of victims went to apply for death certificates. There I saw survivors of the tragedy and worked with them to help process the wide range of feelings—from denial to grief—that they felt. My initial job was to assist individuals make applications for death certificates of their loved ones. In that capacity, I was an escort who walked with families from the front of the building to the back and talked with them about what they were feeling, what they had felt, or what they anticipated doing in regard to the emotions that would be coming. I also accompanied families to Ground Zero so they could see for themselves the honor and finality of the event. The view of the site helped many individuals begin the process of grieving in depth, as they realized in a stark and striking way that those they had loved and cherished in so many ways were indeed dead and would not be coming back to be with them.

From these experiences and other related incidents, I learned a great deal more than I ever anticipated about the nature of counseling, clients, and even myself. In what follows, I will describe what I became most aware of during this time and immediately following. These lessons have some universal application for persons who enter almost any crisis situation. They are especially applicable to crises that may seem on the surface overwhelming.

LESSONS LEARNED

The first lesson I gleaned from my time as a grief and crisis counselor is the realization of how crucial the personhood of the counselor is. I knew this fact going in, but I relearned it time and time again. There are many people who have technical skills that are helpful in times of need. However, in dealing with individuals who are traumatized, the first critical factor that comes to the forefront is the mental health of the person who would be a helper.

A counselor who has difficulty dealing with the rawness of feelings or who is put off with severe emotional pain is unable to function adequately, let alone effectively, in such circumstances. Therefore, it is crucial that in a crisis situation a counselor be ready physically, mentally, and behaviorally. Health within the person of the counselor fosters the ability to reach out in a way that facilitates growth for those in need.

Besides the integrative and healthy nature of the counselor as a person, another essential element of the process of helping in the midst of crisis is in the interpersonal domain. A counselor who tries to do everything ends up not doing anything worthwhile in the short run and becomes a burden to others. Therefore, those who choose to work in crises must quickly build a sense of support through interpersonal relationships with other professionals.

The good news is that such alliances are often easier to forge in these times because of the cooperative spirit among professionals that transcends terrorism and any pettiness that might otherwise be present. That was the case in New York, at least, and I found great strength and wisdom among those with whom I was privileged to work.

Another response to a crisis, I realized anew, is that of flexibility. The circumstances under which clients arrive for assistance in times such as these are not ideal. They arrive in many states of mind. Some are in denial. Some are angry. Others are alone or psychologically separate. To assist them in expressing their grief, mental health workers, such as counselors, must stay fluid in regard to what they do. One has to be ready to deal with anything. Thus being ready to appropriately respond to the novel and unexpected is a necessary requirement for this work that is forced to the forefront of needed skills.

Knowing follow-up resources and persons is a similar needed skill that I realized anew from my work in New York. I was from out-of-state and therefore it was necessary for me to link those I worked with to practitioners and mental health facilities in their own neighborhoods so they would have support after I left and not flounder around without adequate resources.

As professionals, we know we need links to community agencies and specialists. Thus, we gather that data accordingly, and usually gradually. In crisis counseling, the speed at which this task must be completed is greatly accelerated as is its significance.

The importance of small acts of kindness is another point I repeatedly saw in the aftermath of the WTC tragedy. People were appreciative of such gestures in ways that were unexpected. For example, handing clients individually wrapped packages of tissues inevitably brought remarks of gratitude from clients with whom I worked. Words of condolence, such as "I am sorry for your loss" also seemed deeply appreciated. It may well be the brutality that had beaten these people down made them more open and receptive to these simple actions. Regardless, these uncomplicated acts of kindness seem to be beneficial in not only establishing rapport but in starting the healing process.

Nonverbals were essential too. Some of these acts, but by all means not all of them, were received in a different way than anything I have witnessed before. These types of communication took the usual forms such as a touch on the shoulder, support of an arm, or a simple glance conveying empathy.

They also took the shape of giving small stuffed bears or beanie babies to children and their parents as we walked past reminders of those who had died, such as walls with pictures of the missing on them. Regardless, recipients seemed to be deeply touched possibly because of what they were experiencing in regard to sight, sound, and touch. Thus, the nonverbal signals seemed to be picked up gratefully as well as quickly.

The final lesson that comes to mind in regard to my time with families in New York is that of being especially mindful of taking care of myself as a person and a professional. In crisis there is a tendency to sometimes try to display "the hero syndrome," where one does without needed essentials such as nourishment and sleep. While such behavior may yield something in the short run, it is devastating in the long run because the hero ends up burning out, blowing up, or bowing out because of a lack of stamina. There were only a very few people I saw who tried to be heroes like this, although the temptation was tantalizingly available. Instead of yielding to such temptation, I and others found that walking to and from work, writing in a journal regularly, taking needed nourishment, and debriefing with professionals on site enabled us to maintain a positive outlook, maintain our health, and deal with the affect and behavior that constantly came before us.

CONCLUSION

In the midst of working with people who are in a crisis there are a number of important things to keep in mind. Some of these are obvious. Others are surprising. All are essential.

Thus, it is critical that in a New York or other trauma situation that counselors make sure they:

- are mentally healthy to begin with,

- interact in positive and professional ways with colleagues,

- stay flexible and be ready for the unexpected,

- learn resources and people within the community to whom they can make referrals,

- realize the power and potential of small acts of kindness, such as a sympathetic word,

- be mindful of the influence of nonverbal actions that lend support to those in need, from giving them tissues to offering them symbols of comfort such as stuffed bears, and

- take care of themselves through physical exercise, keeping a journal, taking in needed nourishment, and debriefing regularly.

In summary, counseling after a crisis is a time filled with heavy emotion. It is a time of opportunity as well as turmoil. It demands much of counselors. Knowing what to expect can make the experience both positive and productive.

Samuel T. Gladding, PhD, NCC, CCMHC, is professor of counselor education at Wake Forest University.

Reprinted with permission from "Helping People Cope with Tragedy & Grief," published by ERIC Counseling and Student Services Clearinghouse.

3

Joel M. Baker

When I think back upon September 11th, my first thought is about my brother-in-law, Tom. Tom worked for Sandler Oneill, a bond trading firm. He was in the second World Trade Center (WTC) tower. He never expected the second strike to hit his building and when it did, he never had a chance. He was on the 104th floor. Even though he was my wife's younger brother, I had always looked up to and admired him. The pain of losing him is constant. I think of him daily. My wife and my daughter cry for him.

My second remembrance has to do with my work. I am a Student Assistance Counselor at Clifton High School. I am very much a crisis counselor.

When the first plane hit the WTC, the staff and students turned on the news and watched in horror. Soon a multitude of students was in our office. My partner, Joe, and I talked and cried with the students. Joe, although he did not know it at the time, lost a cousin. Students were in a panic. They kept trying to reach a parent or sibling who might have been working in the area of the WTC at the time. I was feeling useless; here I was trying to help students who were in desperate need of reassurance, yet I had to deal with my own fears for my brother-in-law. I felt helpless! I was honest with the students. I told them about my brother-in-law. My wife reported a rumor that he was seen outside the tower but she said she was not sure if it was true. All day long more and more kids kept coming into the office. I could see in their faces that their worlds were shattered. I longed to hear any news about Tom as well. I was so overwhelmed by emotion that I became numb. Here I was in a brand new job and I was helpless and hopeless. I found strength through my partner. I was able to fake it and hide my feeling of ineptitude.

We found out later that day that Tom e-mailed his best friend at 9:07 a.m., leaving him only eight minutes to leave the building. Yet we still had hopes that he was alive.

Back at work a miracle had occurred. We had no fatalities among any immediate student family members. Many kids and their parents made contact with our office to thank us for our help. I felt relieved and happy for the kids that they did not have to deal with a loss.

My family continued to hope that Tom would come home, but he did not. The devastation that our family faced continues. Tom's wife was extremely distraught. Tom's children, Dylan (age 3) and Lukas (age 2), will never really know their father. Tom was the best father to his children. He was at school on Dylan's first day. He attended all the birthday parties that his children were invited to. He was fortunate enough to be wealthy, and gracious enough to give money to worthy causes. Tom also had a younger sister who lived in Manhattan. Within two months, she had quit her job and moved her family to New Jersey.

My daughter, Rebecca, stills talks about Tom. When she was two, Tom wore a Barney costume to her birthday party. He bought her first bike. My daughter idolized him. She still sees the school counselor once a week. In late October, we had a memorial service for Tom at the arboretum in Summit, NJ. We planted a tree in his honor. More than 500 people came to the service. It was a loving tribute to a great father, uncle, son, and brother. Today, I have nothing but great memories of Tom. Like all brothers we had some disagreements but we always looked out for one another. I hope his children will be able to remember him. I know that I'll never forget him.

Joel Baker, MA, SAC, LPC is a Student Assistance Counselor at Clifton High School.

...FROM DORMITORY No. 911, GEORGE WASHINGTON UNIVERSITY, WASHINGTON, D.C.

4

Julia Runte

"Hannah...Hannah...HANNAH!" I yell across the tiny bedroom in Room 911, our apartment-style dorm in the Foggy Bottom section of Washington, DC. As a new transfer I had been there two weeks.

"Jules, it's 8:40, why are you waking me?" During all this talking, our other roommate is still asleep.

"Your phone has been ringing for 10 minutes. I think it's something important." Hannah finally rolls over to answer it.

Moments later she came running back into the bedroom screaming, "GET UP! THE WORLD IS ENDING!"

Veronica and I slowly work our way over to the television and then we are awakened much faster than we had intended when we saw the news. The World Trade Center (WTC) and Pentagon attacks were on CNN and every other channel. We were hysterical and terrified for friends trapped in the WTC, but even more so for people we knew close by at the Pentagon.

Our city was under siege. No channel gave the same information. CNN reported that there was a car bomb at the State Department four blocks from our dorm, and that a hijacked plane was flying over DC and might be shot down. I panicked and did not know what to do. The phones lines were dead. The only way I was able to get in contact with anyone was through the internet.

Luckily my brother was online and he contacted my parents to tell them we were safe. He talked me through my anxiety attack. Chris warned us to gather food, water, and flashlights in case we had to evacuate or go to the parking garages under our building. This made us more frantic. We started running around our little apartment collecting anything we could, which consisted of sweatshirts, tuna fish (the only non-perishable item we had), and water; none of us had flashlights. Who brings flashlights to college?

Seeing our hysterical behavior, our friend volunteered to go down to the lobby to the university police. We were told to stay in our room even though we live in a corner apartment and a hijacked plane might have been circling above us. We huddled in a corner and flipped from one news station to another for the longest time.

We started to calm down as the day went on but we were too scared to leave the dorm. We hadn't eaten anything and had very little food in our refrigerator, so we ordered pizza.. We're college students, it was the only thing we knew. Later on that night, we had to get out. We ventured out and walked to Memorial Bridge. It was a very humbling experience to see one of the most secure places in the world—the Pentagon—on fire. We joined a candlelight vigil and walked for what seemed like hours.

The next few days were extremely nerve-wracking, since our campus is right in the heart of federal district security. Within a 20-block radius are the State Department, all the monuments, the CDC, the World Bank, the International Monetary Fund, all the embassies, and the White House, with Capital Hill not much farther. For safety, hummers were parked on every block with military police bearing rifles. But for a student this was scary. The military police left after three weeks, just in time for heavy security on campus for the World Bank/IMF protests.

Just as life seemed to be getting back to normal, the anthrax scares began. Our mail, and that of the federal district, went through that now infamous Brentwood Post Office. The university was on heightened alert. We were instructed to examine our mail carefully and not to open anything that looked suspicious. Even worse, about thirty-percent of my school is from New Jersey, where much of the anthrax-laced mail had originated. We were afraid to open anything. The

Brentwood Post Office remained closed and we received mail through two small post offices in Northern Virginia and Maryland.

We came to realize that at times like this, you just have to deal with the adrenalin and the fears. But I wouldn't want to be anywhere else.

Imagine being a new student in Washington, D.C. on September 11th. Imagine living in a ninth floor corner apartment with lots of windows. Imagine being in the heart of the federal district with reports of a hijacked plane overhead. When Hannah came running in, we thought she was having a nightmare because she talks in her sleep; but it was real life.

I live in room number 911 and we used to joke about it being the hospital emergency room for our dorm. We pronounced it "9-1-1." Now we say it as "9-11," and each time, the memories of the fear and terror of that morning return.

Julia Runte is a student at George Washington University, Washington, D.C.

Section Two

Responding to Terrorism

Rituals and Creativity: Strategies for Victims of Terror

5

Patricia E. Hudson

Using rituals and creativity as therapeutic interventions may be effective for victims of terror who are resistant to usual trauma therapies or unable to receive or relate to them. These strategies were effective for one counselor educator who worked with victims of the September 11th attacks.

After the World Trade Center (WTC) attacks in New Your City, many mental health volunteers poured into the city offering services to those who were traumatized by the event. Well-trained mental health professionals worked with survivors, rescue workers or those who had lost loved ones. The work they did was admirable, but after a few weeks, they had to return to their homes.

The mental health workers who live in the city were left to deal with another whole group of traumatized persons—school administrators and teachers, NYC office workers, folks who have had their roots here for generations, and newcomers from around the world who came to put down roots in a city they thought was safe. The mental health workers who called NYC home were themselves often traumatized and already worn out and drained. There were far too many people who needed formal services. An added burden was that the mental health workers and counselors had to sustain their own "regular" jobs as well. This chapter describes some of the work a counselor educator did in her own neighborhood after work each day. The rituals helped her and her neighbors heal.

Ritual for an Individual

Ed is a 50-year-old middle management executive who worked on the 15th floor of an office building two blocks from the WTC. He is rather passive in personality, lives by himself, and is an active member of his neighborhood church.

When terror struck on September 11th, he was at his desk doing his routine work. The noise and the panic that occurred two blocks away spread in seconds to the surrounding buildings. Ed had a sense that there was danger for himself and his staff when he heard the news, so he started running for the elevator and called to his staff to come with him. He acted sensibly by instructing them to run from the building as fast as possible. They followed his orders although some doubted that there was an emergency. That changed abruptly when Ed and his companions reached the street and became engulfed in the big black cloud of smoke. After several minutes, the air cleared just enough for Ed to start walking. He made it safely across the Brooklyn Bridge. On the other side, some young neighbors called to him and offered him a ride home.

When Ed arrived home he called no one and felt no need at that time to share his experience with friends or family. He calmly showered, washing off all the soot and ashes that covered him. He washed the clothes he had worned that day, cooked his supper, read for a while, and went to bed.

The next evening, his neighbor (who is a counselor), called to see how he was doing. Ed was very "high" and told about his experiences, as though he had seen an exciting movie, occasionally laughing and suddenly becoming very anxious. His voice was high pitched and he was unusually animated as he talked, waving his hands in the air uncharacteristically.

The neighbor brought him "down" by talking calmly and slowly about what had happened. Over the next few days, Ed related that his brother, who also worked near the disaster, was crossing the Bridge just ahead of him but somehow Ed lost track of him when he reached the other side. Ed did not even look for him. The neighbor took him back to that moment when he realized he could not see his brother any more. Through gentle prodding, the neighbor helped Ed to slow down, take deep breaths, and finally to cry. His guilt at running home without his brother was over-whelming. The tragedy itself, at that point, was not part of the conversation.

Ed was clear that he did not believe in the "psy-chology stuff" being offered on a voluntary basis at his office, yet his need for some intervention was apparent. Ed knew the neighbor to be a counselor and was will-ing to talk to her only as a neighbor. Over the next few weeks, the neighbor just checked in. It was vital to monitor Ed's ability to cope and to determine if family members should be involved in his care or if the coun-selor needed to seek some other assistance for Ed.

Developing an appropriate ritual

After about five weeks, Ed began to think that he had done a terrible thing by washing the soot and ashes off himself and his clothes. He was deeply troubled by the news reports that some bodies would never be found. Due to intense heat of the explosion, it was assumed that bodies were pulverized. He came to the neigh-bor/counselor's house late one evening in a distraught state, saying he had washed parts of bodies down the sink. He felt he had washed away their holy remains and believed that he should have kept all the soot for a proper burial. He then began to assume he had destroyed DNA samples.

In order for ritual to be effective, the client must be involved in the design. The counselor must allow the client to explore what is comfortable, yet must also be creative in assisting the process. Typically, no two rit-uals play out in exactly the same way.

Ed had been collecting newspaper clippings of names and brief biographies of those who were missing. These were the bodies he believed he had washed away.

The neighbor/counselor told him to continue this practice of clipping articles from the newspaper for another week and then bring them to her house.

When Ed arrived the next week, he was reluctant to speak. Together, he and the counselor went to the nearby church where both worshiped on Sundays. The church was empty; they sat near the altar on the floor and talked about the people in the pictures and the possibility of them being alive several weeks after the tragedy. Ed concluded they were not alive. Together they prayed for the people and Ed cried quietly. They then put all the clippings in a container with some incense and burned them. The client and his neigh-bor/counselor sat in silence for a few minutes. When the fire had burned out and only warm ashes remained, Ed took them and buried them in the churchyard.

Ed and the neighbor/counselor have talked rarely about the ritual and at the six-month anniversary of September 11th, they visited the burial place under the shadow of an azalea bush in the churchyard. Ed appears to be doing fine. He reports that the ritual was the turning point in his healing.

RITUAL FOR A GROUP

Many of us assumed that the trauma New Yorkers were experiencing was related to the traumatic event, but that was not exactly the case in one immigrant neigh-borhood. Although American flags were flying every-where, they were a rare sight in this neighborhood. These people had experienced no loss of life at the WTC. Instead it caused them to revisit the trauma of wars, the terror of guerilla armies, and the constant vio-lent internal fighting that forced them to leave their own land. The absence of flags and their minimal inter-est in what had happened in the city divided the local community. A ritual was developed to reunite the com-munity and to provide the people with an opportunity to grieve for their own past losses.

The Catholic Church posted a notice that there would be Tuesday night gatherings with one of the priests and the neighbor/counselor. It would be a time to share experiences. No one would be obligated to speak. The meetings were scheduled to last six weeks and no affiliation with the church was necessary to attend. All were welcome.

Each Tuesday night, several unlit candles were placed on a low table in the middle of a circle of chairs. The group was instructed that they were welcome to speak when and if they felt like it, but they must not ask questions or make comments during or after some-one told their story. It was only a time for listening. After each person finished speaking, he or she lit a can-dle for a person or a place that was affected by violence. The neighbor/counselor assumed the role of facilitator and employed support group leadership techniques. A time limit of one hour was set.

The meetings

The priest, a trained counselor, began the evening with a story about the violence in Northern Ireland, where members of his family live. When he finished, he lit a candle for Northern Ireland. Next, a woman from Ethiopia spoke of violence in her country as her reason for coming to the United States. She lit a candle for her cousin and brother who were killed in a violent attack. The evening proceeded this way with nine of the twen-ty attendees telling their story. At the end of the evening most attendees gathered in small circles, putting their arms around each other and praying for a few minutes. The groups were composed of several cultures and religions from this multicultural neighborhood.

Attendance grew to 36 persons by the final week. The attendees decided they would take their candle home each week, keep it in a special place, and bring it back and relight it the following week.

The final week brought a sense of sadness at the thought of closure. The neighbor/counselor opened the final meeting with a story about her work with persons directly traumatized by September 11th. The group focus turned to that event and concluded with attendees deciding that their experience should make them look outward rather than inward. They committed themselves to becoming more sensitive to coworkers who were traumatized and wounded by September 11th. They talked about teachers and children in the local schools who had lost loved ones. They promised to become wounded healers by listening to other's stories and by praying. As a symbolic gesture, they exchanged candles with each other so they could take them home to remind themselves of the suffering of others.

SCHOOLS DIRECTLY AFFECTED

BY THE ATTACKS

The counselor educator was asked to facilitate a forum for five principals from the schools hardest hit on Staten Island, NY (directly across the Hudson River from the WTC) and one assistant superintendent from NYC. The purpose of the forum, held one month after the attacks, was to discuss the events and strategies they used to cope with the disaster.

Immediate response to the tragedy

The administrators used a range of strategies. Phone lines were dead and disaster plans were either old or not helpful. Administrators had to depend solely on the members of their inhouse staff and faculty. Some of them who had family members working at the WTC or in rescue operations were overwhelmed and therefore could not continue to work. They were relieved of their responsibilities. Others who were in the same position bravely continued their work until the last child was taken home. Not one child was lost or unaccounted for by evening.

• Near the scene of the WTC disaster—Volunteers walked in from the streets and offered to assist the teachers by walking with the children

to another school. The volunteers then delivered notes to the homes, informing parents where their children could be picked up.

• On Staten Island—These families sustained great losses and the children were kept in school until dismissal. Many parents and grandparents rushed to school and, after being appropriately identified, were permitted to take children home. Children who traveled home on buses were sent with additional teachers on the buses. They had instructions to not leave any child at his or her home unless an adult was there to meet them.

• Other schools in New York did a variety of things. In some schools in Queens, the children can see the city skyline, and therefore the twin towers, from their windows. Teachers, traumatized themselves, made children look away, others removed them from the room and still others allowed them to watch and then processed it with them. Some communication via cell phone was established and so a number of teachers were unable to complete the day because of family members who were in the WTC or who were part of the rescue effort.

During the weeks following the tragedy the following activities were designed to assist the children with coping:

High School

• Principals formed advisory committees made up of faculty and students and directed the committees to create activities that would assist all the students in dealing with the tragedy.

• Memorial services were held for those lost or missing when classes resumed.

• One school has a cafeteria message board that had been used to announce after school activities. The principal turned it over to a group of students who created messages each day related to September 11th. Some days it was a simple "God Bless America" and other days it said things like "stay strong" or "we will not give up."

• A group of volunteer students was trained to deal with classmates who had lost family members. The students, accompanied by a faculty member, would visit the family or go to the funeral parlor or attend memorial services and express their support to the grieving classmate. They learned how to sustain that support and were able to process their visits with the school counselor.

- A principal in a private school took volunteer students to the funerals of relatives of other students and then processed it with the students.
- School counselors offered additional time to facilitate groups of students and parents.
- School counselors worked with faculty to identify emerging trauma problems among the students.
- Students made collages that expressed a range of emotions as well as positive, powerful statements. The collages were professionally reproduced and given to the students who worked on them. Copies also were hung in their school. Many said "God Bless America."
- Students wrote sympathy letters to nearby firehouses that had lost several firefighters.
- Students were encouraged to create drawings to express their feelings. Many drawing from small children were of the towers burning. Older children tended more toward drawings that said, "God Bless America" and "I love NY now more than ever."
- A group of students in an alternative school for children with serious problems made very inspiring posters on computers.

Middle School

- Principals in middle schools also formed advisory committees made up of faculty and students and asked the committee to create activities that would assist all the students in dealing with the tragedy.
- Students were encouraged to participate in neighborhood memorial services with their parents. The services were often candlelight processions to a wake or a firehouse or police station.
- A group of children spent time in an after school program writing songs.
- Students made cards for the nearby firehouse.
- Students brought homemade cookies to fire houses and police stations and they continued to do so well after the attacks.
- Students participated in collecting money for the Red Cross and other funds.

Elementary school

- Children wrote stories and drew pictures about their perceptions of the disaster.
- Teachers were given assistance by school counselors and school-based support teams in discussing the disaster and how to deal with the fear generated by the constant showing of the collapse of the twin towers on TV. Many

children experienced each showing as another building going down.
- Guidance counselors formed groups to work with children at all levels and to assess children who needed referrals for further counseling.

All levels (K-12)

- Teachers had several debriefing sessions.
- School counselors had opportunities to get additional training in handling the crisis. Some report that the training became more like a support group because of the needs of the counselors.

Undergraduate students

- Opportunities were presented for students to volunteer at the respite centers, food services or clothing distribution centers. They were accompanied by a faculty or staff member.
- Memorial services were conducted on campuses.
- Campus ministry offices provided gatherings for students to share stories.
- Students were encouraged to talk with counselors on campus.
- Students created appropriate responses within their own organizations.

Graduate School Students

- School counseling students were offered an opportunity to meet with faculty and adjuncts who had expertise in grief counseling
- Counseling student interns gathered information on procedures the schools were using to cope and shared them with classmates.
- Counseling students were invited to a Saturday six-hour training seminar in trauma work.
- Counseling students were able to discuss their personal feelings about the disaster throughout the semester.
- Counseling faculty were invited to a discussion with a police psychologist and a Red Cross volunteer, both of whom had extensive experience working with rescue workers and families at the disaster site.

Aftershock

- No school crisis plan, no matter how recent, was adequate for a disaster of the magnitude of September 11th.
- Communications can be destroyed forcing those in authority to operate on their own.
- Mental health workers and counselors from

around the world respond to a disaster but when they return to their homes soon after, the crisis is handled by their traumatized colleagues who are residents of the area struck by the disaster.

- Although no hard data is available, some administrators of counseling and mental health services agree that those who attended some religious rituals, such as prayer or memorial services or Catholic Masses, are doing better that those who did not. Churches, mosques, synagogues and other houses of worship report great increases in worshippers and members.

- Rituals are effective in assisting a reluctant person to grieve.

- The counselor, sometimes also a traumatized victim, must be especially mindful of his or her own needs, and must be vigilant in not forcing personal "cure all" strategies on the client.

- Children and healthy adults are incredibly resilient.

- The impact on those in the midst of the disaster can never be fully understood by those on the outside.

- Counselors must be prepared for the anger that usually emerges after the deep sadness. There is no predictable timeline for this to occur.

- Fear of future disaster is commonplace.

One typical incident of undergraduate resilience and courage

St. John's University opened a new campus one block from the WTC a few days before the disaster. The staff immediately arranged for students to be assisted by a college uptown. However, when the students started walking uptown on that horrible day, they came to the 59th Street bridge and many decided to walk across it and find their way to the St. John's campus in Jamaica. It took most of the day to get there walking.

When they arrived, tired and with only the clothes on their backs, the University community of staff and students welcomed them with new clothes, space in dorm rooms and counselors to debrief them. Those students remained at the Jamaica Campus for the Fall semester, only going back to collect some of their belongings a few weeks after the disaster. The SJU building downtown was undamaged so it was loaned by the University to the city to use as a respite center for firefighters, police and other rescue workers. Many SJU students then volunteered to work at the site on weekends serving food, doing dishes, and running errands.

Patricia E. Hudson, CSJ, is director of Counselor Education Programs at St. John's University, Jamaica, NY.

DOUBLE DUTY: HOW ONE HIGH SCHOOL'S COUNSELING STAFF COPED WITH TWO TRAGEDIES

6

Marie Bullock, Sandy Esquivel, Paula Keating and Carey Mazzoni

Washington-Lee High School, in Arlington, Virginia, felt the impact of two major traumas during the 2001 – 2002 school year. Located in Northern Virginia, some five miles from the nation's capital, we are a diverse, well-rounded school community. There are over 1,400 students at W-L. Our high school offers programs that range from special education to an International Baccalaureate diploma option.

TERRORISM ON OUR DOORSTEP

Like the whole nation, we were shocked by the disaster of September 11th. Yet, beyond the horror, which was absorbed by the whole country, the day had a particular significance for our students. We are the local school option for high school students whose families are housed on Ft. Myer military base, very close to the Pentagon. Many of our students have mothers and/or fathers who work at the Pentagon. Nothing could have prepared us for the events of that day, not for a seasoned counselor of twenty years, not for a new counselor beginning her second week on the job, and not for the others whose experience ranged in between.

News of the attack on the World Trade Center trickled through colleagues in the counseling office. Upon first hearing the news, the counselors, like the rest of America were unsure if the plane hitting the first tower was intentional or merely an accident. However, by the time the news had dispersed through the school community, the second plane had hit the second tower, and it became clear that it was not an accident. As news spread, televisions in the building were turned on and shock and panic began to set in. What no one knew was that things were about to get personal for these students. Reports continued to flood the newscasts that Washington, D.C. was under attack and bombs had exploded at the Capitol and on the mall. Reports of planes enroute to Washington, D.C. were

being dispersed. Then the report came in that a plane had hit the Pentagon, mere miles from the school.

One counselor explained a feeling of disbelief and numbness coming over her. Another explained her initial thought was of friends who worked in the Pentagon. However, all agreed the immediate priority was the students, and it was necessary to put personal emotions aside for the moment. The counseling department quickly went to work to provide assistance and support for all students, particularly for the many with parents working or stationed at the Pentagon.

As word spread through the school, students began arriving in the Counseling Office. Phones were provided for students to attempt to contact parents at the Pentagon or surrounding buildings. Although initially some of these attempts were successful, the scenario quickly changed, as the phone systems throughout the county became unable to handle the high volume of calls. Calls were neither going out nor coming in. For many students and parents, this now became a time of panic, as contact was now not possible.

Crisis Groups Form

As the situation deteriorated, a crisis group made up of the counselors, school psychologists, and social worker was formed. The team was stationed in the halls, counseling office, and library. Individual crisis counseling was provided by the counselors within the counseling office, in an attempt to calm the increasing number of terrified students. Students were then being sent to different groups that had been set up in the library and run by the school psychologists and social worker. For hours, these efforts enabled students to discuss their growing fears and to receive up-to-date information, as it became available, within a calm and supportive atmosphere. In addition, students were encouraged to continue their efforts to contact parents.

23

Although the school continued to watch the television broadcasts, at times it was difficult to establish exactly what was going on. As counselors, we had to continue to put aside personal reactions and emotions of the horror of this tragedy, and focus on the needs of the students.

Meanwhile rumors of government buildings being attacked, the metro transit system shutting down, and people stranded in Washington, continued to surface. The reality was that the city was being rapidly evacuated as thousands attempted to make their way home. Traffic was gridlocked not only in the city; but also throughout Arlington and Northern Virginia. The streets outside the school, which had already been filled with a constant stream of fire and rescue personnel enroute to the Pentagon, now became gridlocked with cars. Amid the chaos, the superintendent made the decision that Arlington Schools would remain open. It was felt that not only was this the safest and most secure environment for the students, but also that parents may be stranded in traffic, unable to get home to their children for hours.

In Retrospect, What Worked Well
We feel that though this was an event no one could prepare for, having a crisis management team in place helped in handling the situation. Although not age appropriate, we felt it was important to allow students (if they desired) to be able to witness the tragic events which transpired, not in isolation but with caring and supportive adults. This also helped to alleviate feelings of being "kept in the dark" or censored from what was occurring in their own country and in their own lives. Finally, we believe the decision to keep the school open afforded students a safe and protected environment.

SECOND TRAGEDY STRIKES
Our second tragedy would come five months later. During the early morning hours of Sunday, February 3, three of five W-L students, coming home from a party, were killed in a fiery crash not 1/5 of a mile from the school. A senior, junior, and three freshmen were in the car; two of the freshmen and the senior were killed. The two remaining students were in the hospital. The W-L staff was informed of this tragedy, via a telephone network, by the school principal. All staff members were notified prior to Monday morning so that they could deal with the shock before having to work with the students.

Monday morning began with a meeting to discuss what steps would be taken that day. Counselors were stationed in the cafeteria before school began to handle any problem that arose there. During the televised morning announcements, the entire student body was informed of the events, which had taken the lives of three of their schoolmates. There was a school-wide moment of silence in memory of those students. The principal concluded her remarks by letting students know that the upstairs library was available to students who did not feel they could go to class at this time or need to talk to someone about the incident.

Crisis Team Forms Again
A "crisis center" and team, consisting of school counselors, the psychologist, and social worker as well as a grief team (which had been sent in by the central office), had been established. A Director of Counseling Services from a nearby middle school was also invited to be part of the "crisis center" team in order to help ninth graders, who had not yet solidified a relationship with their current counselor. This provided them with a familiar presence to help them through the experience. Senior administrative staff from the central offices were also on hand to ascertain what additional support might be needed.

As students filtered into the library, many sat around tables consoling each other. Initially, counselors just let the students "be," giving them respectful space, but stepping in when it appeared that support was needed. When it was obvious that students were overcome by grief, one of the team members stepped in to give particular support. A major focus was to help kids tell their stories and share memories about the students who had died. Students clustered in groups that had particular ties to each of the students who had died. Students expressed all sorts of emotions, which ranged from extreme sadness to anger at the loss. All of the team took great care not to get into conversations that involved blaming or moralizing about decision-making with the students. This was not the time.

Should We Proceed with Activities Planned for that Day?
All of the counselors were involved in the crisis center. This was made somewhat cumbersome because the scheduling process for the next year was also taking place that day. Counselors were scheduled to be in the classrooms, throughout the day, explaining scheduling to the students. It was decided that the scheduling process needed to go forward, as it was important to maintain as much of a sense of normalcy as possible. Therefore, counselors rotated in and out of the center,

touching base with the students they knew personally. This was a difficult balance for counselors to maintain, their first instinct being to be with their kids throughout the day. In retrospect, however, this worked well. It allowed students to see that even at a time of stress it can be useful to have a normal pattern.

Channeling Feelings is Key

As the morning moved on, it seemed that it would be useful to find an activity to help kids channel their feelings and overt expressions. Banner paper and markers were obtained from the Art department. We asked the kids to help set up tables where students could express feelings of concern and sympathy for the families of the students lost and injured. This activity helped to focus students' energy in a positive way while providing a release for the emotions, which were strongly felt. Kids were told that the banners would be displayed in the school and then given to the families of the students who had died. As word of the banner project spread, some teachers began escorting their classes to the library to write condolences. This was extremely cathartic and helped youngsters feel they had an active part in directing the school's collective grief.

As lunchtime approached, the students were encouraged to attempt to return to class. Some were able to do this; others tried but were not successful.

By afternoon, a handful of students remained in the library. Those students were taken over to the counseling office and gathered in a small group. They were reassured that they could be there as long as they felt it was needed. The two or three that still remained after a half an hour or so, talked quietly. Letters were sent home notifying parents of the situation and explaining services that had been offered to students.

The Next Day

We knew that the challenge would continue the next day. One of our goals was to attempt to get things back to normal, while also maintaining the support. It was decided that all students should be asked to return to classes. On the morning announcements, our principal thanked students for their respectful demeanor the previous day, and asked that all students report to class. Attendance, which had been suspended the previous day, was now required. If a student felt the need to see a counselor, teachers were asked to provide him or her a pass to the counseling office.

It was also announced that Memory Books were being set up in the downstairs library. Pens and index cards were distributed to English classes, in which teach-

ers were asked to allow 15 minutes to students for writing messages or drawing pictures for the books. Teachers were invited to participate also. These books were given to the families of the students after the funerals.

Honoring the Memory

The school made sure that there were representatives at the funeral services. Watching kids say goodbye and helping them deal with wrenching separation is more than painful. Yet, for all of us, it was one of the most important parts to be played.

Students were asked what student-directed activities they would like to organize to honor the memory of the students who died. It was stressed that although the deceased were part of our school community, they were first and foremost family members. All ideas were respectfully discussed and considered, yet some (such as pictures on tee-shirts) were set aside when students realized that family members might be upset to suddenly see a picture of their son or daughter in a mall. Ideas that were accepted included: a memorial flower garden around the school sign, dedication of the yearbook, and a moment of silence at graduation.

Other things that we would do again include: provide cookies, lollipops, and bottled water for the students; make sure plenty of tissues are available (a run to the store was necessary to replenish the supply); provide memory books as a way to help kids express their deep emotions and thoughts; attend funerals and memorial services; give kids some space to just "be"; be respectful of each and every idea; and, Listen, Listen, Listen.

TEAMWORK: THE MOST VALUABLE LESSON LEARNED

As a school, we are still aware of the deep scar that we bear from this year's events. We know that reminders of these days will be poignant at times such as prom, yearbook signing, and graduation. However, as in all things in life, we have taken some valuable lessons with us. We have learned that as a counseling department, we work in concert with one another. We have learned (or have been reassured) that our students are resilient and caring. We have learned that we can depend on one another, and in fact, we need to know we can.

Marie Bullock, PhD, is Director, Counseling Services at Washington-Lee High School in Arlington, Virginia. Sandy Esquivel, MA, and Paula Keating, MEd, are counselors at the school and Carey Mazzoni is a counseling intern.

Jill Riethmayer

How does one explain the unexplainable to children? How can adults expect children to comprehend what adults themselves cannot understand? While adults are still reeling in shock from the September 11th attacks, those very adults are expected to offer explanation, strength, and support for the children of local communities and states across the country. For many adults, this task has been far too difficult—due, in part, to where the adults have been "emotionally" in response to the attacks. What is the role that counselors can play in assisting children to acquire the knowledge and tools needed to live successfully in this new era of terrorism on American soil?

FOREIGN WORDS: "WE ARE AT WAR"

First, counselors, as well as parents and educators, must remember that as "foreign" as these terrorists attacks on American soil (and the new war on terrorism) were to adults, they were far more foreign to children. When children first heard in President Bush's address to the nation, "We are at war . . .," they were hearing those words for the very first time in their short lives. To children, those words were a foreign vocabulary, an abstract concept, as well as a frightening reality. Also for the first time, children as well as many adults in the U. S. saw the following:

- Activation of the National Guard and Reserved Armed Forces on a large scale
- Streets patrolled by the National Guard
- Every airport in America closed for approximately one week
- Armed guards in those airports once they were reopened
- Fighter jets sent to ward off more air attacks (even at entertainment events)
- Anthrax-laden mail

The day of the attacks, as well as the days following the attacks, have been described by many adults, as well as children, as resembling destruction that had previously been viewed only in movies showing mass destruction, such as in the film Independence Day.

How children cope with what happened on September 11th depends to a large degree upon the adults around them. Adults must provide the response model for children.

THE ISSUE OF SAFETY

Paramount in working with children in response to the new terrorism threat is to recognize that the perceived sense of national safety once felt is now gone. In the past, children always believed that America, as the most powerful nation in the world, could protect its citizens —especially its children. After September 11th, the children of the U.S. had to face and accept the new reality that America is not "safe" from terrorists. Indeed, the very targets of the attacks were national symbols of strength: the World Trade Center (financial strength), the Pentagon (armed services strength), a possible attempt to destroy the White House (presidential strength) and/or perhaps the U.S. Capitol (national government strength).

Two things need to be addressed in relation to this new realization of loss of safety. First, children will need to grieve a loss in a safe and peaceful country and world. Even though this sense of national safety was merely perceived by many children, as well as adults, the fact remains that after the attacks, this nation is no longer a "safe" nation. The loss of that secure and care-free sense of safety needs to be identified, processed, and grieved by children. Second, children will need help in defining a "new normal." The normal life that existed prior to September 11th does not exist. It has been shattered – both literally and psychologically. What must be done for the children is to help them define a new normal—the post September 11th "normal."

THE NEED FOR INFORMATION

One of the major needs of both children and adults was, and still is, a need for knowledge and accurate information about terrorism—what it is as well as what it is not. Terrorism is the intentional psychological trauma to the living with the primary goal of ruining the hearts and hopes of those people. In contrast to what is commonly believed, killing people and producing mayhem are only secondary goals of terrorism. It is a willful and planned psychological assault against the hearts, minds, and spirits of a large group of people—in this case, the people of the U.S. It is intended to inflict continuous psychic injury to thousands and perhaps even millions of people—all at the same time. This "psychic infection" is far more destructive than any biological or germ warfare. The infection that terrorists hope to circulate through the veins of the victims is this: innocent people become afraid of life, innocent people become afraid of the future; innocent people put off the living of "life"; and that innocent people move about more cautiously.

The list below provides simplified information that may be helpful in explaining terrorism to children:

Terrorism 101

Terrorism is:
- acts of violence, abuse, murder, and destruction against unsuspecting people, groups of people, or nations by individuals or groups of people

Terrorists believe:
- that their cause is more important than human life or property
- that their feeling of "being right" is greater than even their own life

Terrorists' goals are:
- to create terror (main goal)
- to create destruction (smaller goal)

Terrorists can be:
- big or small
- white, black, brown, or any color
- American or from any nation

Terrorism produces trauma, which is:
- an out of the ordinary event
- scary, difficult, shocking, and possibly life-threatening
- a feeling that creates fear, sadness, and anger

THE THREATS OF TERRORISM

In working with children, the counselor must keep in mind the many different kinds of threats that children have experienced in regard to the attacks of September 11th. First and foremost was the threat of life—the fear and threat of losing life, limb, or health—either the child's own life or that of someone the child loves.

The second form of threat was a world-view threat. Children were forced to encounter human evil. That raised the question of why innocent people have to suffer and it challenges the idea that the world is safe, kind, fair, predictable, and trustworthy. The third form of threat was a self-ideal threat. This event caused children to act, think, or feel in ways that contradicted their views of themselves and what others expected. For many, it caused a regression in thinking and behaviors. Children might have felt humiliated by the intense feelings of helplessness and fear as well as the fact that they did not function as well as they wished they had.

The fourth threat is the emotional stability threat. Children may have become frightened not only of the terrorists' threat, but also of the "bomb" of feelings building inside of them that might go off at any time—perhaps unexpectantly. The fifth threat is the threat to thinking and logical abilities. Children may have trouble getting along with others, concentrating, remembering and completing tasks. As the child becomes aware of this difficulty, he or she may become even more anxious and less functional; anxiety produces more anxiety.

The sixth threat is that of breaking the parent-child "relationship." Implicit in the parent-child relationship is the expectation that parents will always protect their children. Because parents could not protect their children from these attacks or from the Oklahoma City bombing, or Columbine High School shootings, children may feel betrayed or even abandoned by the parent as well as angry at the parent. Some children even fear that if their parents found out how disappointed and angry they were, then the parent might reject or abandon them.

The final threat is the threat of intensification of current, nontraumatic stresses and difficulties in the life of the child. Trauma can make ongoing problems more difficult to deal with and it can bring up old, unresolved trauma. The most vulnerable children prior to September 11th were those who had experienced a loss recently (Matsakis, 2001).

Guidelines for Discussions

- Assume children have heard about it; the child usually has more knowledge than the adults assume.
- Be available and approachable—let the child know that it is okay to talk about unpleasant events.
- Clarify the question so that it is clearly understood what is being asked as well as understanding what led to the question: curiosity or fear.
- Treat all questions with respect and seriousness no matter how difficult or silly the question might seem to an adult.
- Tell the child the truth as clearly and honestly as possible, making sure to use developmentally appropriate language and definitions.
- Do not be afraid to say, "I don't know."
- It is okay to tell the child that the counselor needs more time to think about his other question.
- Accept the child's reactions, and reassure the child that his reactions are common and okay. Help to normalize the child's feelings.
- Be aware of magical thinking. Does the child believe he or she caused it?
- Share your feelings; this models expression of feelings for the child.
- Affirm to the child that he or she has survived the trauma.
- Reassure the child; help the child feel safe.
- Identify what the adults in the child's world are doing to restore safety as well as to protect the child from future trauma.
- Help reestablish a sense of order through returning to normal routines, family time, etc.
- Monitor media coverage and restrict it—be aware of vicarious trauma.
- Watch for symptoms of feelings that go beyond fear to anxiety.
- Remind the child that in response to the September 11th trauma, the U.S. has much support from around the world.
- Remember, adults serve as role models for the child.
- Support the child's concern for people he or she does not know.
- Help the child find an outlet for thoughts, feelings, and desire to help.

Age Has An Impact on Reactions

Remember that a child from one age group will react differently to the same trauma than will a child from another age group. Listed below are the major age groups, needs, and appropriate responses.

Early Childhood and Preschool

Response: Even though very young babies and toddlers may not know what is transpiring in the world, they may pick up a parent's anxiety with their own sixth sense. The child may appear very confused by these events and may have difficulty separating media images from reality.
Needs: Calming, normalcy, protection, soothing, holding, and hugging

Elementary School Children

Response: The child is much more aware of both what is going on as well as the reactions of other people.
Needs: Honest talk, emphasize safety, limit media, return to normal routine, provide outlets for expression.

Middle School

Response: The child is extremely aware of what is going on in the world and may be prone to exaggerating. This age group often uses jokes and humor to mask real fears.
Needs: Honest talk, comfort and reassurance, wants details

High School

Response: May act like he or she does not care, but this is often an attempt to look strong and to "save face." Has probably already talked about the attacks with friends. May remain glued to the television, eager for breaking news and details.
Needs: Honest talk, ease feelings, engage in serious discussion

Young Adult

Response: The young adult will have more realistic fears. Will tend to focus on the cause and may want to take some kind of action such as getting in a car and driving to a vigil, etc. May begin to question the value of chosen areas of studies and/or jobs in terms of what is really important in life.
Needs: Guidance in directing the young adult into positive outlets. Provide an opportunity to engage in serious discussion about not only the event, but the changes that follow in the life of the young adult as a result of the trauma.

WHAT COUNSELORS CAN DO

The way in which a school and school counselors respond to children will have a major impact upon how well the children cope after the trauma. The first priority is to establish a sense of safety and security for the child. The closer the child is to the actual trauma, the greater this need is.

Children often will take on the anxiety of adults around them. Try to distance adults who are overly anxious from direct contact with children. Provide initial as well as ongoing opportunities for the children to talk about what has happened as well as to express their feelings. Encourage expression of feelings to adults, teachers, or parents who can help the child understand the strong and sometimes troubling emotions that follow a trauma. Help children understand that there are no "bad emotions," and that a whole range of reactions is normal.

Educate the child about what to expect following a major trauma. While helping the child to identify and express feelings, provide reassurance that their feelings will get less powerful and easier to handle over time. Do emphasize though that it will take time. Treat all children's fears as genuine even though the fears may appear unrealistic. Do not ignore the need that children have to talk about what happened as well as about any loss or death that may have occurred.

Throughout the process of working with children, try to place the attack in perspective. In addition to the tragic things that children have seen, help the children identify good things that have come out of what has happened. Examples are: heroic actions of ordinary citizens; police personnel, emergency personnel and fire fighters getting long deserved recognition for selfless service to the public; families who are more appreciative of each other and who are grateful for having been spared and/or reunited; recognizing that family is more important than making money; the goodness of people around the country and world who responded with help; and the renewal in patriotism as well as a greater appreciation of the freedoms enjoyed in the U.S.

What About PTSD?

Although many children will display some symptoms after a trauma, only a minority will develop post-traumatic stress disorder (PTSD) symptoms. A study in response to the Oklahoma City bombing found the following:

- Children who lost an immediate family member, friend, or relative were more likely to report immediate symptoms of PTSD than other children.
- Arousal and fear were significant predictors of PTSD symptoms seven weeks after the bombing (Pfefferbaum et al., 1999).
- Two years after the bombing, 16 percent of children who lived approximately 100 miles from Oklahoma City reported significant PTSD symptoms related to the event (Pfefferbaum et al., 2000).
- PTSD symptomatology was predicted by media exposure and indirect interpersonal exposure, such as having a friend who knew someone who was killed or injured.
- No study specifically reported on rates of PTSD in children following the bombing. However, studies have shown these statistics regarding percentage of children who develop PTSD: as many as 100 percent of children who witness a parental homicide or sexual assault, 90 percent of sexually abused children, 77 percent exposed to a school shooting, and 35 percent of urban youth exposed to community violence.
- Due to the nature of the WTC attack, a very high rate of PTSD is predicted for children who lost a family member or witnessed the plane crashes or the aftermath. Based on research from Oklahoma City, a high rate of PTSD may also be related to exposure to media coverage and to children who have a friend or family member who was killed or injured.

SIGNS TO WATCH OUT FOR

Dr. William Steele, founder of The National Institute for Trauma and Loss (2001) in Children, identified these indicators of problems:

- Has trouble sleeping, afraid to sleep alone, or to be left alone for short periods of time
- Is easily startled (terrorized) by sounds, sights, smells similar to those that existed at the time of the trauma
- Becomes hyper vigilant—always watching out for and anticipating that he or she is about to be in danger
- Seeks safety spots in the child's environment
- Becomes irritable, aggressive, acting tough, or provokes fights
- Verbalizes a desire for revenge
- Acts as if the child is no longer afraid of anyone or anything. In the face of danger, the child

responds inappropriately, verbalizing that nothing ever scares them anymore
- Forgets recently acquired tasks
- Returns to behaviors the child had previously stopped
- Withdraws and wants less interaction with friends
- Develops headaches, stomach problems, fatigue, or other ailments not previously present
- Becomes accident prone, takes more risks, or puts self in life threatening situations
- Develops school problems, including a drop in grades and difficulty concentrating
- Develops a pessimistic view of the future, losing resilience to overcome additional difficulties, losing hope, losing the passion to survive, play, and enjoy life

If these indicators are observed in a child, it is critical that the child receives assistance in working through the trauma. Children most at risk are children who have unresolved old losses and/or unresolved previous traumas. The new trauma—in this case, the terrorist attacks—will activate the pain of the old, buried, ungrieved trauma and losses.

The role that adults play in assisting the child in understanding and processing the attacks of September 11th is critical. Children will naturally look toward adults for answers and guidance on how to respond to the "unknown." In order to be an appropriate model for the child, the adult must be: available to the child physically and emotionally; knowledgeable about trauma as well as terrorism; open to the child's expression of strong and often confusing feelings; and, sensitive to the child's critical need for comforting and support. It is also necessary for the adult to have worked through his or her own issues regarding the event.

How does one explain terrorism and the terrorist attacks to a child? The answer is one: one question at a time; one feeling at a time; one reassuring look, touch or word at a time; and one "normal" day at a time.

References

Matsakis, A. (2001). *Helping children cope with trauma.* Retrieved January 1, 2002, from http://www.mataskis.com/helping_children_cope_with_trauma_for_parents_and teachers

Pfefferbaum, B., Nixon, S., Tucker, P., Tivis, R., Moore, V., Gurwiten R., Pynoos, R., & Geis, H. (1999). Posttraumatic stress response in bereaved children after Oklahoma City bombing. *Journal of the American Academy of Child & Adolescent Psychiatry,* 38, 1372-1379.

Pfefferbaum, B., Seale, T., McDonald, N., Braqndt, E., Rainwater, S., Maynard, B., Meierhoefer, B., & Miller, P. (2000). Posttraumatic stress two years after the Oklahoma City bombing in youths geographically distant from the explosion. *Psychiatry,* 63, 358-370.

Steele, W. (2001). Terror on top of trauma reactions in children. Retrieved April 22, 2002 from http://www.survivorguidelines.org/articles/steele01.html

Jill Riethmayer, LPC, NCC, LMFT, is Director of The Center for Student Assistance, Blinn College, in Bryan, Texas.

Using Metaphor to Help Children Cope With Trauma: An Example From September 11th

8

Maureen M. Underwood and Charles Clark

The use of metaphor to help both children and adults cope with difficult challenges in life is not new. Myths and fairy tales chronicling a hero's struggle against formidable odds were passed down through oral tradition even before written language was invented. Current school curricula is replete with "message stories," which are often designed to help children problem solve more efficiently, understand the multifaceted dynamics of human interaction, or appreciate the complexities of life. While these stories address the general range of human issues that children and adults most commonly face, the events of September 11th were so unprecedented that finding appropriate stories that captured both the devastation as well as acknowledged the challenges of change has been difficult.

The need for such metaphor was particularly acute for the children who lost a family member on September 11th. It was critical to find a story that directly addressed an event that might be perceived as traumatic to a child, while providing a reasonable amount of emotional distance from the reality of that particular day. It was also important that the mental health concepts of cognitive restructuring and resiliency be included as models of coping strategies for the children and families who had suffered such traumatic losses. Having the story be "reader friendly" was another critical variable in story selection. The mental health education embedded in the story needed to be accessible to an audience without a background or perhaps even an appreciation for mental health. The story also needed to appeal to children who were not directly touched by the events of September 11th but who are now living in a culture that is permanently marked by the residual anxiety of those events.

Rather than search for a story that met those criteria, the authors decided to write a story of their own. The writing team consisted of a clinical social worker with a practice specialty in crisis intervention for children and a construction engineer with no formal mental health training. This pairing was an intentional strategy to facilitate the translation of mental health concepts into every day language. The gender of the authors corresponds to that of the two main characters, a middle school boy and girl who are best friends. The incident described evokes the total destruction of September 11th, albeit in story book form, and the solution incorporates both cognitive restructuring and science in a concrete demonstration about how to view disaster in a totally different way. The story is part of a series called "Adventures on Maple Street" that involves the same two main characters and addresses similar themes. While the series was originally written for incorporation into a structured group curriculum being conducted in New Jersey with families who lost a member on September 11th, the authors feel that it is generic enough to be adadpted for use with other populations as well.

The Story: "THE SNOW GLOBE"

Even when I was a little kid, I learned that life can teach you some amazing lessons.

I remember when I woke up that morning years ago, I had a hunch it was going to be a perfect day. The sun was streaming in through my bedroom window, the birds were singing outside, and it was Saturday. And it wasn't just any Saturday—it was my best friend Maggie's birthday.

Now I know it may seem kind of weird for a kid like me to have had a girl for a best friend, but Maggie wasn't like most girls. She liked snakes and lizards, and could even skateboard better than me, which is saying a lot! And if that doesn't convince you how cool she

33

was, how about the fact that she named the family's sissy little dog "Dirt Ball?" I rest my case.

So you can imagine that I wanted to get someone as cool as Maggie a really neat birthday present. I'd been thinking about what to get her a long time and when we went to the mall with my mother, I'd paid close attention to the things Maggie said she liked. She looked at some baseball stuff in the sports store and some books about raising snakes for fun and profit in the pet shop, but it was all pretty ordinary. It wasn't until we walked past this artsy place that she stopped in her tracks.

In the window was this giant snow globe. Inside the globe, there was a girl sitting on a rock, surrounded by a bunch of animals. At the top of the globe, there was a sun in the sky with a rainbow behind it.

"Oh, can we go in and see it?" Maggie begged, and of course my mom said yes.

The saleslady had to take it out of the window since it was the only one in the store. "This is a very unusual snow globe," the saleslady explained to us, as she lifted it carefully from its perch. "If you look at it the way it is now, it's a daytime scene. But when you shake it up, look what happens." The saleslady turned the globe over, shook it a few times, then set it upright again. Magically—I have no other explanation for it—the sun became the moon, the rainbow turned into the Milky Way and gold glitter blanketed the sky like a million shooting stars.

"Amazing," my mom said.

"Wow!" said I.

Maggie was just speechless.

It was a pretty pricey present on a kid's allowance, but I promised my mom I would do extra chores if she'd loan me the money to get the snow globe for Maggie's birthday. Would I really do the extra chores? You probably already figured out the answer to that question. Did I get the snow globe anyway? Aren't moms great?

So my mom wrapped up the snow globe in this terrific blue paper with stars and moons on it. Then she tied squiggly ribbon all around it, and it looked as amazing outside as I knew it was on the inside. "Be careful carrying it," she warned me as I left the house. "It's fragile." I mean, like she really had to tell me to be careful. Sometimes my mom was, well, such a mother! When I got to Maggie's house, her dad answered the door.

"Hi, Sport," he said to me. Like, did he really think that was my name or did he just forget my real one? "Maggie's in her room. Go on up."

"Hey, Mags," I yelled, as I started up the stairway. "Wait till you see your birthday present." I didn't want to ruin the surprise, but I was pretty excited about it myself. And I couldn't wait to see her reaction.

"Hey, Creep Face," she called as she burst from her room. "What you got for me?"

What happened after that isn't really clear in my mind. It was like when you watch a movie and you know what's going to happen next and you want to yell at the hero and tell him "WATCH OUT!!" And you do yell, but you get this sinking sensation in your stomach because you know it's not going to change the terrible thing that's about to happen.

What I do remember is Maggie running out of her room, me running up the stairs, and Dirt Ball getting in the middle. When I tripped over him, his collar somehow snagged a strand of that squiggly ribbon and flipped the present out of my hands. It went tumbling slow motion into the air, out of my reach and even beyond the reach of the now wide-eyed Maggie. My disbelieving feet were frozen to the floor as I realized in horror I was not going to be a hero and save the present but, even worse, maybe I wasn't even going to still be a best friend. The crash of the present on the hardwood floor shocked me back to reality. The snow globe's fluid was already leaking through the starry wrapping paper, dashing any slim hope I still had that the world had not ended.

Maggie bent down end ripped open the paper. Her face fell when she saw the picture of the snow globe on the bent and soggy box. By now, the glitter was seeping through the cardboard and pooling on the floor. "Oh," said Maggie, "Oh."

I suppose I might have felt better if she'd yelled at me for being so careless, but Maggie just sat there, taking the broken pieces one by one from what remained of the box. She set them carefully on the floor beside her. The rainbow was in three pieces, and part of the little girl's dress had broken off. The animals were shattered, and the sun had disappeared.

"I'm so sorry, Maggie," I croaked, my voice on the edge of tears. "I've broken your wonderful snow globe."

"Well Henry, you're right. It's not exactly wonderful now," she replied in her most grown up voice. Maggie hardly ever calls me by my real name. When we were babies I used to like to play with these toys called "creepy crawlers" and Maggie gave me the nickname "Creepy." Over the years it morphed into "Creep Face." Actually, I kind of like it since it reminds me that I've known Maggie my whole life. Nobody but

Maggie gets to call me that and I'm so used to her saying it that I get kind of freaked when she uses my real name. And she never uses my real name unless I'm in some kind of trouble.

I was really on the verge of tears now but somewhere in the distance I heard Maggie continue. "But I've got something that may make things better," she said. "Wait here."

In a flash, Maggie was up from the floor and dashing down the hall, Dirt Ball racing behind her. She was back in less than a minute, holding a small worn-looking tube with what looked like a clear glass marble stuck in one end. "This is another present I got for my birthday," she informed me, "from my Grandmother Joanna. It's called a taleidoscope."

"A what?" I asked, now feeling both careless and stupid at the same time.

"A ta-lei-do-scope," she repeated slowly. "Here, let me read what my Grandmother wrote on the card that she sent with it."

"My Dearest Sweet Maggie," she read as she winked at me. "As an almost grown up young woman who has just about everything new an old grandmother could think of giving her, I decided my present for your birthday this year would be something that belongs to me. Your grandfather gave this gift to me many years ago, and as you can see from the condition it's in, I have made good use of it. It's called a kaleidoscope. I know you know what a kaleidoscope is, since I gave one to you and your brother for Christmas several years ago.

A taleidoscope is similar in construction, but instead of looking at a container with brightly colored things inside, you look through the lens at everyday objects that are multiplied and transformed into miraculous treasures. I always enjoyed looking at anything that was interesting to me through the taleidoscope lens, because I found that these things were even more fascinating when they were arranged in spectacular designs. On days when I felt bleak and dreary, a few minutes with my taleidoscope always helped me remember to look at what was troubling me in a different way. So, sweet granddaughter, this gift gave me both pleasure and a new view of the world around me. May it bring the same to you."

Maggie finished reading and looked up at me. "It's from your Grandmother Joanna?" I asked. "The one who's at least 120 years old?"

"I know, Creep Face," Maggie answered, "her ideas are usually a lot old-fashioned. So let's put this thing to the test." She rolled the taleidoscope around in her hands for a few seconds, then put it up to her eye. Her reaction was immediate.

"Oh," she exhaled. "Ohhhhhhh."

With her eye glued to the lens, she slowly turned the cylinder and continued to gasp. "What is it. Maggie?" I was worried, thinking a second gift was about to bite the dust.

"Here, look!" she exclaimed, gently placing the taleidoscope in my palm. "You are not going to believe it."

With more than a little apprehension, I raised the cylinder to my eye and aimed it at the mess on the floor. This couldn't be! Instead of the broken snow globe, I was looking at billions of dancing stars, comets of red and green instead of the girl's broken dress, and deep blue starbursts instead of the soggy wrapping paper. With each rotation, the picture became even more magical, especially when I looked at the pool of glitter on the floor. Before my eyes, it transformed into firework bursts of golden diamonds. Now, I was speechless!

We took turns admiring the wreckage on the floor until Maggie's mother called from the kitchen to remind us it was time for lunch. Reluctantly, we trudged to the kitchen for grilled cheese sandwiches. Maggie carried the taleidoscope with her.

Maggie's mom eyed the cylinder next to Maggie's plate with a touch of envy. "Been looking at things upstairs?" she asked quizzically. Maggie mumbled an answer between sandwich bites.

Her mom continued, "I remember looking through that thing when I was your age," she said to Maggie, "and I was always so amazed at how different the world looked through that lens. Even ugly things were transformed."

"Like you, Creep Face," Maggie said to me as she polished off her sandwich and turned the taleidoscope to look at me. "You are some kind of beautiful!" she laughed.

By the time I left Maggie's for home that afternoon, the catastrophe with the snow globe seemed far behind. It wasn't until my mother asked me how Maggie had liked her present that I began to think about everything that had happened that day.

"She liked it fine," I told my mom "But she got this even neater gift from her Grandmother."

It's been a lot of years since that day when I was sure both the world and my friendship with Maggie had ended. Actually, Maggie and I are still close friends and it seems impossible that we are already in high school. She doesn't seem to have the same interest in snakes and I've begun to notice that she's kinda pretty and that FINALLY I am taller than her. In science class we were studying about light, and Mr. Taylor, my teacher, used a taleidoscope to illustrate some experiment. That reminded me about that day at Maggie's house. You know, I still feel a little sad about it—that snow globe was so unusual and had seemed so important. But I've never forgotten the lesson Maggie's grandmother gave us in her message about the taleidoscope and I often think about seeing the patterns of light and hope beyond the sadness and the mess. The amazing thing I learned that day has stayed with me all these years. When I remember to be like a taleidoscope in looking at the world, especially at the times when life doesn't seem to make much sense, the goodness and beauty are always still there.

DISCUSSION QUESTIONS

The following questions are suggested for classroom or group discussion of the story. They ask the listeners to put themselves into the story and think about and process their own feelings. They also elucidate cognitive restructuring techniques, emphasize the value of incorporating older adults into one's support system, and invite children to identify an issue in their own lives that they'd like to be able to view in a more positive way.

1. Could you understand why Creep Face got so upset when he broke the snow globe? If this had happened to you, how do you think you would have felt?

2. Creep Face says it might have been better if Maggie had gotten angry at him when he broke her present. Why do you think he says that?

3. How do you think Maggie felt laying all the broken pieces on the floor? What do you think was going through her mind at the time?

4. Why do you think looking at the mess through the taleidoscope helped Creep Face and Maggie?

5. Have you ever been in situations in your life that you looked at in a different way? What were they and how did seeing them differently help?

6. Maggie got the taleidoscope from her grandmother, and both she and Creep Face seem surprised that an older person would know what a kid would like. Are there any older people in your life who seem to really understand what kids like and need? Tell a story about one.

CONCLUSION

Although this story was written specifically to help children reframe the events of September 11th, the authors feel it might be even more helpful if used proactively to reinforce coping techniques for children in advance of difficult life circumstances. There are many events in life that can feel like the end of the world to children, and remembering to view them in a different way can make them easier to bear.

Maureen M. Underwood, ASCW, LCSW, is the coordinator of a group practice in Morristown, New Jersey. Charles Clark is President of Clark Construction Company.

The American Red Cross: How to be Part of the Solution, Rather than Part of the Problem

9

Howard B. Smith

Following the events of September 11th, many American Counseling Association (ACA) members and professional counselors wanted to volunteer their services through the American Red Cross (ARC). Some were turned away; others were asked to take a two-day course before they would be allowed to volunteer. Some thought this was an unnecessary barrier that kept them from providing a much-needed service. This chapter provides the rationale behind these perceived barriers and explains how to be prepared for assisting in a disaster.

The ARC authority to perform disaster services was formalized when the U.S. Congress chartered the organization in 1905. This authority was reaffirmed by federal law in the 1974 Disaster Relief Act (Public Law 93-288) and in the 1988 Robert T. Stafford Disaster Relief and Emergency Assistance Act. Stated slightly differently, the ARC has both a legal and a moral mandate to provide disaster relief, and furthermore, it has neither the authority nor the right to surrender that mandate. It has both the power and the duty to act in a disaster. The organization receives no governmental funding; it depends solely on the generosity of the American people to fund its entire operation.

In 1994, ACA signed a Statement of Understanding (SOU) with the ARC committing the two organizations to work together in these ways:

- Encourage state and local administrative units of each organization, with guidance and direction from their national units, to engage in training and exercises as appropriate.

- Ensure that ACA will provide volunteers to assist in disaster relief operations, especially in the Disaster Mental Health and Family Services functions of ARC.

- Offer the appropriate ARC training to ACA members who are licensed or certified for independent practice by a governmental agency, and wish to volunteer in the Disaster Mental Health Services (DMHS) function. This training would make them eligible to respond to nationally declared disasters.

To meet its obligation, ACA has, for the past several years, offered the DMHS course as a pre-conference course. At the 2002 conference in New Orleans, ACA offered two sections and trained 41 ACA members. A third section could have been added, given the widespread interest. In late 2001, ACA President Jane Goodman contacted the ACA state branches and encouraged them to work with the lead chapter of ARC in their state to sponsor training for ACA members. And, as part of my responsibilities as Associate Executive Director for Professional Affairs, I serve as the liaison to the ARC on behalf of ACA. These are just some of the ways ACA is working with the ARC.

ADDITIONAL SKILLS NEEDED IN DISASTERS

Based on my personal experience as an ARC volunteer over the past 10 years in several disasters, including the Pentagon and World Trade Center, I offer these thoughts. Providing mental health services in a disaster environment requires an additional set of skills that are noticeably lacking in counselor education programs. That skill set, in brief, includes the ability to apply clinical skills in an environment where chaos and lack of organization prevails, to concentrate on getting individuals to an acceptable level of functioning quickly following traumatization, and applying these skills in a systemic manner for the benefit of all. To accomplish this, counselors must have: good physical and mental health, an understanding of and an appreciation for other facets of a disaster relief operation, and a willingness to be flexible while working as a member of a team.

Why is licensure or certification required?

To protect itself from lawsuits, ARC policy requires of its mental health volunteers licensure or certification by a state governmental agency for independent practice. The ARC could have legal exposure if it allowed unlicensed professional counselors to perform services under the auspices of the ARC. Ours is a litigious society, and the last thing the ARC wants to do is to spend the donations from the American public on unnecessary lawsuits. The Disaster Mental Health function of the ARC is one of only two functions for which licensure or professional credentials are required. The other is Disaster Health Services. Nurses and physicians who volunteer their time also must be appropriately credentialed.

Unlicensed counselors can play a role

An excellent way for unlicensed, professional counselors to provide volunteer service is by becoming a Family Service Worker. These individuals are on the front line with people, helping them obtain monetary assistance for immediate needs such as food, clothing, shelter and other necessities. While this work is not officially considered "mental health" care, clearly, a person with a high level of listening skills, sensitivity, and overall ability to help clients would be a valuable asset in any disaster. Training is required for these volunteers.

Even licensed counselors must be trained

The rationale for requiring the additional training for licensed mental health professionals is a bit less straightforward. A mental health professional who provides services in a disaster environment does, in fact, need all of the clinical skills they gain in their formal education and in supervised clinical experience. That preparation, as invaluable as it is, is not sufficient when working with clients who have experienced the type(s) of trauma and loss that result from natural and man-made disasters. In addition to those finely honed clinical skills, the mental health professional needs an understanding of and appreciation for the entire disaster relief operation system. Without this training, one might make what appears to be a clinically sound recommendation regarding the services available or where to go to get the services needed. In a disaster, individuals need a bit of structure that they can depend upon. To misinform a person in the midst of crisis would only add to the confusion and disorientation. Furthermore, to appear at a disaster without this training and expect to get it "on-site" would burden other mental health professionals.

The ARC course entitled "Introduction to Disaster," a pre-requisite for the Disaster Mental Health Services course, provides an introduction to the disaster environment and to the other components or functions of the ARC that are part of the response delivery system. This information is critical for those who want to work within the Red Cross on a relief operation. Knowing what services are available and how to access them is vital. That information can do wonders to relieve the client's stress and anxiety in a disaster.

Providing disaster mental health services in the chaotic environment is different from seeing clients in an office. A typical encounter in a disaster may take place while the client is rummaging through the ruins of their home or while they are waiting to see a Family Service Worker who will determine the extent of their immediate needs, or while they are standing in line to get a meal from the Emergency Response Vehicles. Counselors and other mental health professionals must often initiate conversations based on their professional assessment of a person's needs at the moment. An intervention may consist of a 15-minute conversation in which the client is assured that what he or she is feeling is a normal reaction to a set of abnormal circumstances. Does this mean that all of the client's emotional or psychological needs have been met or addressed? Not any more than applying a tourniquet to stop the bleeding means that a bodily wound has been adequately cared for. It is but one, albeit a vitally important, step in the person's recovery from a disaster. It is mental health first aid.

The longer-term issues that often arise in a disaster, such as the death of a loved one, obviously require appropriate longer-term care. Within the ARC system, this is provided not by the Disaster Mental Health Professional but rather by a licensed practitioner in the community to whom the client is referred. These are individuals who have volunteered to do disaster-related mental health counseling on a pro bono or reduced rate basis. The purpose of the mental health care function of the ARC is not to compete with local practitioners, but rather to fill a disaster-caused void of services by meeting the immediate mental health needs of the clients with highly trained and credentialed professionals.

Having excellent clinical skills is a very good beginning for those who wish to help in the aftermath of a disaster. But those skills must be accompanied by knowledge of the ARC system. Otherwise, the well-meaning professional could end up contributing more to the chaos than to the resolution.

Howard B. Smith, NCC, CCMHC, LPC, is Associate Executive Director for Professional Affairs for the American Counseling Association.

THE BEST LAID PLANS: WILL THEY WORK IN A REAL CRISIS? 10

J. Barry Mascari

Several years ago while planning a workshop on preparing for sudden loss in the schools, one of my colleagues said, "Most people don't plan to fail, they fail to plan." Although we can never be certain that our plans will unfold as smoothly in a real crisis, being prepared always yields better results than being unprepared. Planning for a crisis is what this chapter is about. The practical tips offered will help to make your experience easier.

WHAT IS A CRISIS?

The term *crisis* is overused in our language; however, there are true crises and we need to agree on a definition. In order to be a crisis, the incident must:

1. Affect and distress many people (as opposed to an individual in crisis)

2. Be unexpected (has the element of surprise)

3. Be a "disaster" (of varying magnitudes from a single family to large numbers of people)

4. Involve some type of loss (death, serious property loss, destruction of a community symbol)

5. Disrupt normal routines

6. Make people feel "out of control" or uncertain about the future (fear, loss of structure and predictability)

7. Not go away overnight (people will not feel better about this in the morning)

The September 11th attacks on the World Trade Center (WTC) and the Pentagon met all the above criteria for a crisis:

1. Many people died; many were involved or witnessed the events on television
2. It was unthinkable before September 11th
3. (see #1, above)
4. Many deaths, huge property loss, symbols of American economic power destroyed, the financial center of the nation, if not the world, attacked
5. There was a constant stream of news on the television. Disruptions were everywhere: communications, media, air travel, local travel, parents not coming home
6. The sense of vulnerability, the lack of clarity about exactly who was responsible and what would happen tomorrow
7. Media coverage was incessant, loved ones were missing, air travel was disrupted, and it was nearly impossible to get back to normal.

During my 20 years as counselor and a District Supervisor of Counseling and Student Services, I have directed the implementation of crisis plans in the following instances:

- Student shootings after a "battle of the bands"

- Disclosure of sexual abuse by a school psychologist with 20 years in the district

- A "gangland style" murder of a student by two other students

- The death of a popular high school vice principal

- An apparent suicide of the senior class president two weeks before graduation

- An accidental shooting of a student by her husband

- A middle school student killed by a car near the school

- The death of an elementary school student who accidentally hung himself while playing

The proportion of crisis varies with each event. There are several instruments that are helpful in assessing the degree of trauma from a given incident. Oates (1988) developed a useful instrument for "Determining the Degree of Trauma." The instrument (see Figure 1) is not very complicated and provides a quick way to assess the situation. After studying the instrument and using it a few times, it is easy to make an assessment without consulting the instrument.

Planning for the crisis

There are three components to crisis planning:

- Developing a plan before an incident

- Developing activities to implement during the crisis

- Anticipating and planning for what will come after (often referred to as mop-up)

Counselors new to crisis response work typically make two critical mistakes:

1. Failure to put closure on the response process after the event is "over"

2. Being blindsided by the aftermath and its effects on all parties involved

Therefore, the individual(s) responsible for implementing the plan must simultaneously consider the entire process of managing the crisis. In any crisis situation, there is a degree of uncertainty about what will happen next and how long each phase will last. It is helpful to use some type of planning chart. In 1998, with several colleagues, I developed the Sudden & Violent Loss Planning Continuum (Figure 2) to help counselors respond more effectively to what is called the event. The chart includes these phases:

Before (planning)

During (the event)

- Beginning: Initiating the intervention plan
- Middle: Responding and adjusting interventions as the team meets
- End: Closing activities and returning to normalcy*

Aftermath (team debriefing and preparation for delayed responses, anniversaries, and pressure to memorialize the event).

Normalcy is a relative term. After an event, the everyday routines return but the individuals are changed in some way forever. They will never return to the way they were before the event. That is not to say that they are unhealthy, just different. Sometimes they are even healthier after this experience. The point is that everything will not return to "normal."

The Before phase of planning involves readiness to act and an insurance that the response will be swift and orderly. Ask these questions:

Do we have a written plan?

Does everyone have a copy and have they read the parts affecting them?

Does everyone know their responsibilities in advance?

Does the plan cover all contingencies and varying types of crises?

Have we trained staff members who will be involved in any phase of the response?

Who calls whom? (initiating the emergency call-up system, using a helpful chart to organize yourself). See Figure 3, Underwood and Dunne-Maxim (1997).

Who is in charge of what? For example, who will handle the press?

How fast can we mobilize the team?

What if we need help? Outside of the team, who can we call? Who can we count on?

(Being involved with community agencies, hospitals, etc. can pay off during a crisis.)

Avoid confusion by using the 3 RS:
- **Read** about crisis and intervention materials
- **Write** a clear policy and procedure with steps or flow charts
- **Rehearse**

Responding to a Crisis

This chapter does not cover clinical skills for crisis intervention, but it does provide helpful hints on how to prepare for the experience. Regardless of the skill level of the counselors, the following are the accepted keys to an effective crisis response:

- Support
- Control
- Structure

Underwood and Dunne-Maxim (1997) expanded the work of William Worden in identifying four grief tasks as they apply to schools.

1. To accept the reality of the loss.
2. To work through the pain of the loss.
3. To adjust to an environment in which the deceased is missing.
4. To emotionally relocate the deceased and move on with life.

A very helpful statement was offered by the Red Cross during their Disaster Mental Health Response Training. They said that most people in a disaster are:

Normal people - Experiencing normal responses - To an abnormal situation

Six Steps to Being Prepared

By following the steps identified below, counselors will be better prepared to respond.

1. Acknowledge your own fear

Crisis work is frightening, and the uncertainty of it all makes even the most seasoned veteran apprehensive. Remember to breathe! During times of stress we often forget to take deep breaths, which leads to even greater stress.

2. Initiate your response EARLY

Meet with your faculty and teams before school starts. Using the emergency call-up procedure, schedule a meeting before the students arrive to ensure that everyone has the same information about the event. Have any statements, handouts, details, or other information that you wish to share available at this time. This is also the time to prepare and send letters to parents and consider distributing a newsletter (see Figures 4-6).

3. Speak with one voice

Be sure that the district designates one person to speak with the press. Be prepared for the press to criticize the school and to interview students who may not be the best representatives of the school. The police can be particularly helpful in sealing off the campus from the press.

4. Know why you are making any intervention

The team should always understand the goals of any intervention, and their responses to students should be coordinated and consistent. In addition, the team needs to provide structure, support and security.

5. Remain flexible

Be prepared to adjust responses and plans. Meet with your response team daily, or more frequently if needed, in order to keep your "finger on the pulse."

6. Get back to normal as soon as possible

Normalcy and routine help people feel in control. Children especially respond to routine; it reduces their anxiety. (On September 11th, we asked our teachers to keep televisions and radios off, and to continue teaching. This more than anything prevented panic.) Check on the staff members who may have trouble carrying on as usual.

WILL THE PLAN WORK?

There is no good answer to this question, although it is one that we all ask. Below are some possible answers.

No. . . and Yes. Some things will work as planned, others will not. It is the nature of a crisis. For example, although you may have planned to avoid memorializing an event or death, a spontaneous gesture by peers may result in an instant memorial. Students once decorated a deceased student's chair in the cafeteria as a memorial.

It depends. Success is dependent on many factors out of the counselor's control. The American Red Cross reminds Mental Health Response Workers to be flexible, flexible, flexible. It is best to deal with the events you can control rather than focusing on those out of your control.

Define "work." Will it work like clockwork? No. Will you help a great deal of people? Maintain order? Prevent things from spinning out of control? Yes.

Some additional points to bear in mind:
Keep expectations reasonable. This is not about perfection. The objective is to maintain a safe, secure, and orderly environment. Expect that things will not go exactly as planned, or as desired.

Realize that no one escapes these events without a scratch. Things will happen. Plans will unfold differently. When the response is over, your energy supply will be depleted and you will need some time to recover. Helpers absorb a great deal from those who were helped.

Crisis planning is like exercise, it is the cumulative effect over time that matters. The more crises you experience, the better you will get at responding. Better does not mean perfect. It means being more experienced, less nervous, more willing to accept imperfection, and feeling good about what has been accomplished.

It will be better than it would have been without a plan. Be kind to yourself. You have done your best to think of every possible contingency. You are still better off than you would have been with no plan. After the event is over you will be very happy that you had a plan, regardless of how things went.

Aftermath
Helping the helper is one of the most important tasks in any plan and also the most overlooked item. Surveys of response staff indicated the following:

- 87 percent were affected emotionally

- 93 percent felt debriefing was necessary

Most crisis response specialists recommend some type of emotional ventilation within 24 to 48 hours after the response is completed. Debriefing helps everyone get their own lives back to normal. Mitchell (1983) developed the Critical Incident Stress Debriefing (CISD) model, which involves a process several hours in length with multiple questions. The following are the most important issues to be addressed:

The American Red Cross requires that all disaster response workers be offered debriefing (see Figure 7) as a means to put closure on the response experience

and to help return to normal.

If you are the leader of the response team, consider bringing in another professional to lead the ventilation or debriefing session. This will allow you to participate in the debriefing more effectively.

The main point is to stop worrying about whether the plan will work. Once the crisis response is initiated there is barely time to breathe. Remember that you have made a real difference; that should be enough.

J. Barry Mascari, MS, LPC, NCC, CCMHC, MAC, is District Supervisor, Counseling and Student Services, Clifton Public Schools, and he is Chair of the New Jersey State Professional Counseling Licensure Board.

References
American Red Cross (1998). *Disaster Mental Health Services*, Washington, D.C.: American Red Cross. ARC 3043.

Mitchell, J.T. (1983). When disaster strikes - the critical incident stress debriefing process. *Journal of Emergency Services*, 8, 36-39.

Oates, M. (1988). Responding to death in the schools. *TACD Journal*, Fall.

Underwood, M., & Dunne-Maxim, K. (1997). *Managing sudden traumatic loss in the schools.* Piscataway, NJ: University of Medicine & Dentistry of New Jersey.

Additional Resources
Clayton, L.O. (1990). *Assessment and management of the suicidal adolescent.* Dallas, Texas: Essential Medical Systems.

Deskin, G., & G. Steckler. (1997). *When nothing makes sense.* Minneapolis, MN: Fairview Press.

Dudley, J. (1995). *When grief visits school: Organizing a successful response.* Minneapolis, MN.: Educational Media Corporation.

Dwyer, K., & Osher, D. (1998). *Early warning, Timely response: A guide to safe schools.* Washington, DC: U.S. Department of Education.

Lystad, M. (1988). *Mental health response to mass emergencies: Theory & practice.* New York: Brunner/Mazel.

Figure 1
Determining Expected Degree of Trauma

Step 1: Circle the number(s) in each triangle beside any word or phrase that describes this death. Total circled numbers within each triangle.

Step 2: Add triangle totals. Then add one point for each additional person who died or was critically injured in this event to determine a GRAND TOTAL: _____

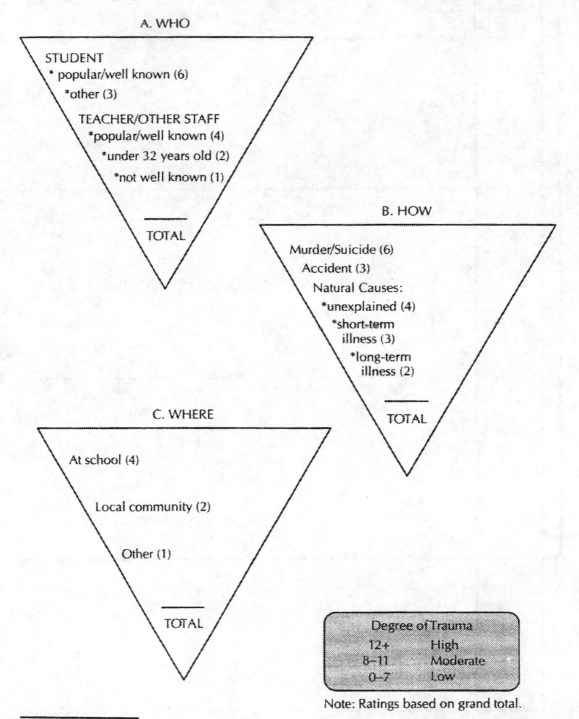

A. WHO

STUDENT
* popular/well known (6)
*other (3)
    TEACHER/OTHER STAFF
    *popular/well known (4)
    *under 32 years old (2)
    *not well known (1)

___ TOTAL

B. HOW

Murder/Suicide (6)
Accident (3)
Natural Causes:
*unexplained (4)
*short-term illness (3)
*long-term illness (2)

___ TOTAL

C. WHERE

At school (4)

Local community (2)

Other (1)

___ TOTAL

Degree of Trauma	
12+	High
8–11	Moderate
0–7	Low

Note: Ratings based on grand total.

From "Responding to Death in the Schools" by Martha D. Oates, 1988. *TACD Journal, 16.* Reprinted by permission.

Figure 2.

SUDDEN & VIOLENT LOSS PLANNING CONTINUUM

EVENT

Before (Planning)	Beginning (Initiating)	Middle (Responding/ Adjusting)	End (Closing)	Aftermath (Team debriefing & memorializing?)

Cascade Campus (handwritten)

01172411   Last updated: 10-25-04 Created: 10-25-04 Revision: 1

01 ACQ TYPE: v   08 CODE3: -   14 ORD NOTE: -   20 STATUS: o
02 LOCATION: eca   09 CODE4: -   15 ORD TYPE: f   21 TLOC: -
03 CDATE: -   10 E PRICE: $34.95 16 RACTION: -   22 VENDOR: amac
04 CLAIM: -   11 FORM: -   17 RDATE: -   23 LANG: eng
05 COPIES: 1   12 FUND: fbed   18 RLOC: v   24 COUNTRY:
06 CODE1: d   13 ODATE: 10-25-04 19 BLOC: v   25 VOLUMES: 1
07 CODE2: 1
26 SELECTOR   mk

B2352107   Last updated: 10-25-04 Created: 10-25-04 Revision: 1
01 LANG: eng   03 LOCATION: none   05 BIB LVL: m   07 SUPPRESS/T: r
02 SKIP: 0   04 CAT DATE: -   - 06 MAT TYPE: a   08 COUNTRY: vau

01 001   50002832
09 003   OCoLC
10 003   OCoLC
11 005   20041025185022.0
12 008   020607s2002   vau   b   000 0 eng   cam a
13 010   2002074578
14 016   7 101154774|2DNLM
15 020   1556202253
16 040   DLC|cDLC|dc#P|dNLM
17 043   n-us---
18 049   OREU
19 050 00 HV6432|b.T472 2002
20 060 00 2002 L-644
21 060 10 WM 170|bT328 2002
22 245 00 Terrorism, trauma, and tragedies :|ba counselor's guide to
           preparing and responding /|cedited by Debra D. Bass and Richard
           Yep.
23 260   Alexandria, Va. :|bAmerican Counseling Association, |
24 300   158 p. ;|c28 cm.
25 504   Includes bibliographical references.
26 650   0 September 11 Terrorist Attacks, 2001|
27 650   0 Terrorism|zUnited States|xPsych
28 650   0 Victims of terrorism|xCou
   650   0 Crisis intervention
   Stress Disorder

Cascade
Campout

Figure 3.

COMMUNITY CRISIS PHONE TREE

INCIDENT

POLICE

Chief: _____	Phone: _____
Alternate: _____	Phone: _____
Alternate: _____	Phone: _____

CALL SCHOOL SUPERINTENDENT

Supt: _____	Phone: _____
Alternate: _____	Phone: _____
Alternate: _____	Phone: _____

CALLS BUILDING PRINCIPAL(S)

Prin: _____	Phone: _____
Prin: _____	Phone: _____
Prin: _____	Phone: _____

[Note: expanded list may be appended]

CALLS CRISIS TEAM LEADER(S) (CTL)

CTL1: _____
Phone: _____
CTL2: _____
Phone: _____
CTL3: _____
Phone: _____

[Note: expanded list may be appended]

CALLS MENTAL HEALTH CONTACTS

Name: _____
Phone: _____
Name: _____
Phone: _____
Name: _____
Phone: _____

CALLS CRISIS TEAM MEMBER(S) (CTM)

CTM1: _____
Phone: _____
CTM2: _____
Phone: _____
CTM3: _____
Phone: _____

CALLS CLERGY & COMMUNITY AGENCIES

Contact 1: _____
Phone: _____
Contact 2: _____
Phone: _____
Contact 3: _____
Phone: _____

Figure 4. Sample letter - Student death.

Dear Parent or Guardian:

The recent death of one of our students has both shocked and saddened the community. In our own way, each of us experiences a search in order to make sense of such an event. Children's grief takes on many forms, and the school has made professional support staff available to assist them in addressing their concerns. We thought that you would like to know about this and be prepared to address unexpected questions or fears, which are children's normal responses to death.

The death of someone outside the family presents an opportunity to begin addressing, in an age appropriate way, the experience that everyone must face at some time during the life cycle. This is an opportune time to share your views on death, especially in the context of family, religious or spiritual beliefs.

Although the issue of death and grief may have been addressed in the classroom in a general way, we cannot offer a view which would include all possible religious, cultural, and family perspectives.

A topic such as this can often strengthen or make closer the parent-child relationship. If you find it difficult to begin the discussion and need some help, please feel free to call me at the School_____ office for further information. You may also want to consult with your own spiritual guide for advice in instructing your child in the context of your belief system.

I am sure that you share the school community's heartfelt expression of sympathy to the family. Your support and cooperation during this difficult time is appreciated.

Sincerely,

Figure 5. Sample letter - September 11th.

Dear Parent or Guardian:

The recent events in New York and Washington have made all of us, but most importantly children, uneasy. I am writing you to offer some simple suggestions about ways that you may make this period easier for your family.

Expect the unexpected from your children, which may include problems with sleep, being excessively "clingy", or having angry outbursts; they are responding differently because their world has changed. You can help them by:

- listening or responding to their behavior without punishing or criticizing them (remember that children respond differently and some may have a delayed response)

- limiting the amount of television news they see you watching, or are actually watching themselves (information is important, but overload can be detrimental)

- assuring them that they are safe and that their life has resumed normalcy (do all of the things that you would normally do)

- making contact with friends, your clergy, or counseling services

Should you have any concerns and wish to speak with a counselor in the schools, either contact the Principal or your student's assigned Counselor. Staff are prepared to make referrals to local counseling centers which are available to help families deal with possible loss.

I am sure that you share my heartfelt expression of sympathy to all of those people who lost a family member. As always, I appreciate your cooperation during this difficult time.

Sincerely,

Superintendent of Schools

Figure 6.

CLIFTON PUBLIC SCHOOLS

Department of Counseling & Student Services

973.470.5697   September 22, 2001

A Parent's Guide: Talking to Your Children About the September 11 Tragedies

Counselors are here to help you, your child, or to find resources

Educational Support Counselor assignments by school

Schools #1, 12 Annex, 16:
Ms. Shawna Ebner-470.5697

Schools #2, 14, 15:
Mrs. Mirta Lopez-470.5697

Schools #3, 8, 9:
Ms. Kathleen Reilly-470.2466

Schools #4, 5, 13:
Mrs. Anne Friedland-470.5697

School #11:
Ms. Gayle Blake-779.5441

School #12:
Mrs. Sharon Santostefano-591.6824

District Supervisor
Mr. J. Barry Mascari

"..in moments of crisis, the American spirit shines forth as courageous, dauntless, and enduring."
— Senator Joseph Biden

Helping Children Cope

The following are offered a guidelines to help you assist children in responding to the recent tragic events.

• **Identify & come to terms with your own feelings first** before helping your child. Helping children put what we feel inside into words helps healing. Anger, shock, & disbelief are common initial reactions. If they linger, seek help.

• **Accept & validate all feelings expressed by children** by using reflective listening saying "I know that you are angry and its ok to feel that way...". Reassure them that what they feel is normal; even adults feel this way.

• **Tolerate their need to review the events over & over.** This type of process helps adults & children come to terms with tragedy. Be patient...

• **Adult grief frightens children, so help them respond.** Children can be frightened by adult grief reactions (even on TV). Tell them crying is the body's way of releasing intense emotion & that they can comfort others in the same way they are comforted when crying.

• **Limit TV accounts & be sure to ask them how they feel about what they saw.**

• **Maintain or return to a normal routine.** Structure & order help maintain feelings of safety & control.

• **Be careful about whom we blame.** It is the government's responsibility to determine who is guilty.

• **Action helps people feel better.** Collecting items, money, making donations, giving blood help us all increase feelings of power & control over our lives.

[The above adapted from *Helping Children Cope With National Tragedy*, a bulletin issued by the University of Medicine & Dentistry of NJ's Behavioral Healthcare centers.]

Figure 6 (continued).

Internet resources for assistance

National Association of Secondary School Principals -
http://www.naspoline.org/NEAT/terrorism.html

Dr. Koop.com, Parenting & Children's Health - Talking with your kids...
http://www.drkoop.com/dyncon/article.asp?ptu=true&id=9683&at=

American School Counselor Association -
http://www.schoolcounselor.org (School Store for parents)

American Counseling Association -
http://www.counseling.org

American Psychological Association -
http://www.apa.org

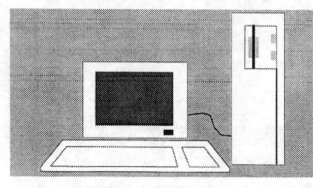

Help young children put their fears in perspective

•help them feel personally safe
•help them understand that precautions are being taken to prevent future terrorist acts
•help them feel in control by taking action (send letters, cookies, or magazines to relief agencies involved)
•if a family member is going to be away, plan activities to minimize the child's fear (keep them busy & reassure them that travel is safe)
•plan a special time (say a half-hour) just for that child and let them know it is "their time"
•expect difficulties at night, especially around bedtime
•ask children what things they need to feel safe (involvement fosters a sense of control)

Ways to help...

•Give Blood: 1.800.GIVE LIFE
•Volunteering-NY State Emergency Management Office: 1.800.801.8092
•Medical professionals willing to volunteer:

    Physicians: 212.604.3850

    Nurses: 212.604.8474

    EMT & Nurses aides:
        800.628.0193

    Search & rescue professionals:
        www.nasar.org

•For donations visit the internet for the 9-11 fund or contact your local chapter of the American Red Cross.
•Volunteer at an organization not related to the Trade Center attack - it helps children find meaning at any time!

Figure 7. Disaster Mental Health Services

DEBRIEFING

Target Group: Red Cross staff, community disaster victims, emergency responders

Intervention: A debriefing—
- Is a discussion of facts and feelings surrounding one or more stressful events. When conducting a debriefing, it must be recognized that multiple stress reactions may arise following a disaster. These reactions may continue for weeks, months or years, as long as the person is involved in disaster response or recovery.
- May deal with acute, delayed or cumulative stress from a single stressor or multiple stressors.
- May be held at any time during the disaster response or relief operation, at the end of a worker's assignment, when the worker returns home from an assignment or at the beginning of a new assignment.
- May be conducted with individuals or with groups. If conducted with a group, all participants may have been involved in different response or assigned to different disaster relief operations.
- Provides education about normal and abnormal stress responses and about methods for identifying and practicing coping strategies.

Ground Rules:
- Participation is not mandatory.
- Groups should not include both victims and workers or workers and supervisors *unless the precipitating event* (such as the death of a shelter resident) had an equal effect on everyone, and the group being debriefed had no opportunity for action. Unless they are also part of this group, supervisors should be debriefed separately from workers.
- All participants must be present for the full session, and interruptions are not allowed.
- If anyone leaves the room, a facilitator will accompany the person.
- Strict confidentiality is observed, and no note taking is allowed. Members of the group may speak to other persons outside the group only about their own feelings and reactions, not about those of others. If any subsequent action is initiated by a facilitator (based, for example, on reported difficulties with a particular staff member), the source of information about the difficulties is not disclosed unless permission is given to do so.

Note: Facilitators have an obligation to state to the group the legal limits of confidentiality, according to applicable state laws, concerning any member who is suicidal or homicidal, or who is suspected of child or elder abuse.

- Criticism of the feelings or reactions of others is not allowed.
- All participants must agree to ground rules before the debriefing session can begin.

Limits: A debriefing—
- Is not a critique of a disaster operation or other workers.
- Deals with facts, feelings, and emotions of those present at the debriefing, not others, although general information may be given about other possible emotions participants may face.
- Does not deal with long-term or chronic problems.
- Is not intensive or individual therapy.
- Is limited to education about adaptive and maladaptive stress responses and coping methods.

Figure 7 (continued).

Format:
1. Identification of the purpose of the group.
2. Discussion of ground rules.
3. Identification of stressful events.
4. Sharing of feelings and reactions associated with the events identified.
5. Discussion of physical, emotional, and cognitive symptoms that have developed or that may develop.
6. Education about adaptive reactions to traumatic events and constructive coping strategies.
7. Information about anticipated future stressors and about methods to cope with them.
8. Question-and-answer period.
9. Closing, with referrals and plans for follow-up as necessary.

Recommendations and Referrals:
1. The group leader may wish to work with individuals to provide additional support or refer those individuals to other DMHS staff for individual assessment and possible crisis intervention.
2. Following individual assessment, the group leader may refer individuals who exhibit an inability to cope or function to community mental health providers/services.
3. All individuals who exhibit symptoms of major mental illness will be referred to community mental health services or, with DMHS supervisory concurrence, to the emergency department of a local hospital.

Possible documentation required when working with individuals following a debriefing:
Disaster Staff:
- *Health Record* (Form 2077).
- *Disaster Crisis Referral* (Form 6641).
- *Release of Confidential Information—Red Cross Staff* (Form 5854A).

Victims:
- *Client Assistance Memorandum* (Form 1475).
- *Disaster Registration and Case Record* (Form 901).
- *Disaster Crisis Referral* (Form 6641).
- *Release of Confidential Information* (Form 5854).
- *Health Record* (Form 2077).

Emergency Responders:
- *Health Record* (Form 2077).
- *Disaster Crisis Referral* (Form 6641).
- *Release of Confidential Information—Red Cross Staff* (Form 5854A).

HOW A SCHOOL DISTRICT CRISIS RESPONSE TEAM CAN HELP

11

James J. McCarthy

Glen Rock School District is located in a small town that is bounded by two railroad lines linking the borough to New York City. Many people in the community board NJ transit trains each day to commute to the NYC financial district. So when tragedy struck on September 11th, our small community was seriously affected, and we continue to deal with residual effects. The magnitude of this tragedy had an immediate impact on our schools. Would we have enough trained staff to cover all of the needs? Of course the answer was No. This would be the case for most Bergen County school districts.

Coincidence can sometimes be the greatest impetus for change. As luck would have it, members of our school staff had been invited to a Bergen County Administrators Conference on "Crises Response" on September 12. The conference speaker proved to be dynamic, and, due to airline restrictions, was trapped on the east coast. This proved to be most beneficial to North Jersey high schools as a session on crisis management was held the next day at Glen Rock High School. Any administrator, counselor or child study team member who wished to attend was welcome. Approximately 14 school district public and parochial personnel attended the program. The conference helped the school personnel with the crisis at hand but also, it set the groundwork for a program to respond to traumatic, tragic situations in the future.

Out of this conference arose the concept of a Bergen County Flight Team, a group of nine schools loosely associated, whose purpose was to have similarly trainer counselors who would be available to respond to crises in each other's schools. The Flight Team planning group identified areas that the team would need to address, and they developed a philosophy, action plans, and response strategies. Here is how the Bergen County Flight Team functions:

The role of the school board in crisis response planning:

- become educated about the need for crisis response planning
- support and encourage your district to plan for and respond to crisis
- promote community awareness and involvement

The role of the district administrators:

- educate and involve your board
- activate the Flight Team for your school or district using the procedures provided by the Bergen County Flight Team Coordinators
- recruit Crisis Response Training participants in the future
- form a building team (at least some of whom receive crisis training)
- coordinate involvement of parents and community resources
- facilitate Flight Team response if members are called to your building
- provide ongoing support and follow-up after a crisis, utilizing team effort to help school regain normalcy
- encourage good self-care for staff and for yourself
- investigate curriculum needs (especially in regard to suicide)

The role of Flight Team members:

- present overview of concept to chief school administrators
- provide a "concept" session to interested administrators
- provide specific recruitment practice suggestions

53

that support a working model over time
- facilitate training in the areas of loss and the grieving process
- assist in the creation of district crisis plans
- network with local resources (Mental Health, Youth Services Team, counselors)
- develop generic crisis plans to be used when a district has no plan
- coordinate crisis response to schools (work with other Flight Team members, organize response, troubleshoot)
- organize parent meetings in concert with district staff
- support the debriefings and support meetings for Flight Team members

WHAT IS A FLIGHT TEAM?

Our Flight Team is made up of 40 trained professionals from the schools and districts listed above. In their "regular" positions, these individuals are counselors, administrators, and members of Child Study Teams. These team members were sent from their schools and districts to receive special training in crisis management and intervention. The flight team concept is used in many states to provide a school or district with large numbers of well-trained professionals when an incident or crisis occurs in a school community.

When and how to contact the Flight Team?

In the past, flight teams have been activated to deal with student suicide, the death of a student or staff member, terminal illness, and earthquake. Other examples that might indicate activation of the Flight Team are sexual or physical assault or serious injury, the witnessing of a traumatic event or any event that polarizes,

isolates or shocks people (such as the arrest of a staff member for a crime). These are the kinds of events the Flight Team can respond to, but each crisis is different, and the decision to seek outside help must be reached following an evaluation of student needs.

Any staff member may approach the principal or a building Flight Team member to discuss the level of response needed. The principal will determine if a Flight Team intervention is indicated and will contact the Flight Team Coordinator.

Functions of the Flight Team:

- assists building administration in crisis management procedures
- provides information to staff on coping strategies
- provides Quiet Rooms for students and/or staff in crisis
- monitors and counsels students/staff in need
- fills in for building staff so they can deal with the crisis
- makes referrals and networks with the community
- follows up by contacting parents, attending funeral, etc.
- assist in organizing/planning school memory activity
- attends to small details so building staff can handle critical items
- helps develop a follow-up plan

James J. McCarthy is principal of Glen Rock High School, Glen Rock, New Jersey.

INTERVENING WITH SCHOOL STUDENTS AFTER TERRORIST ACTS

12

Gerald A. Juhnke

Elementary middle, and high school students witnessing or experiencing terrorist attacks can experience negative residual psychological effects such as post-traumatic stress, generalized anxiety, and adjustment disorders. This paper describes a modified family debriefing model which can be used by mental health professionals affiliated with schools or working with school age children to address needs and concerns of students and parents alike.

INTERVENING WITH SCHOOL STUDENTS AFTER TERRORIST ACTS

Terrorist attacks on civilians in New York City and Washington, DC, and the continued threats of terrorism via biochemical acts and further violence have the potential to engender negative psychological effects such as post-traumatic stress, generalized anxiety, and adjustment disorders upon school age children and their family members. School counselors and mental health professionals working with school age children need to be knowledgeable regarding interventions which provide opportunities for students to openly discuss immediate and future concerns, cumulative stressors resulting from on-going terrorist threats, and post-terrorism psychopathology (e.g, anxiety, distress). Thus, the intent of this paper is to familiarize readers with basic Critical Incident Stress Debriefings (CISD), succinctly outline the distinct differences between CISD and the Adapted Family Debriefing Model for school students, and describe how mental health professionals can use this Model as a post-terrorism response intervention.

CRITICAL INCIDENT STRESS DEBRIEFING VS. THE ADAPTED FAMILY DEBRIEFING MODEL FOR SCHOOL STUDENTS:

Critical Incident Stress Debriefing (CISD) is a widely recognized, small-group process originally developed to be used with adult emergency workers (e.g., fire fighters, emergency medical technicians) who encounter particularly distressing situations (Mitchell & Everly, 1993). This seven-stage model uses adult peer facilitators. Some have cited CISD as a viable intervention with school age children and adolescents who experience violence or suicide (O'Hara, Taylor, & Simpson, 1994; Thompson, 1990). Yet, CISD was originally developed solely for adult use and did not take into account the special developmental cognitive, physical, and emotional needs of school-age children and their families. The Adapted Family Debriefing Model for school students, however, was developed as an assessment and intervention method specifically designed for elementary, middle, and high school student populations exposed to violence (Juhnke, 1997). Compared to CISD's single group experience, the Adapted Family Debriefing Model for school students requires two separate debriefing experiences. The first debriefing experience is with students' parents and does not include students. The second is a joint student-parent debriefing experience.

Additionally, unlike the traditional, adult CISD process which utilizes nonprofessional, adult peer facilitators, the Adapted Family Debriefing Model for school students requires the use of trained mental health professionals who have specific knowledge regarding childrens' developmental needs and an appropriate graduate degree which included clinically relevant courses and internship experiences. Mental health professionals using the Adapted Family Debriefing Model for school students should be familiar with the social, intellectual, and psychological development stages corresponding to the students being served.

DESCRIPTION

Roles. The primary team member roles within the Adapted Family Debriefing Model for school students

55

are leader, co-leader, and doorkeeper. The leader briefly explains the debriefing process, creates a supportive milieu, identifies those experiencing excessive levels of emotional discomfort, and directs team members via hand signals to intervene with distraught students or parents. In addition, the leader discusses with parents and students common symptom clusters experienced by children who: (a) have personally experienced terrorist acts or have suffered loss as a result of such acts (eg., the death of a grandparent or sibling resulting from terrorism), (b) have witnessed via the media terrorist acts or the aftermath of same, (c) understand the potential for continued terrorist acts, or (d) experience the cumulative effects of multiple terrorist acts. Specifically, the leader discusses relevant, depression, post-traumatic stress disorder, adjustment disorders, and generalized anxiety disorder criteria. The leader normalizes manifest symptoms and encourages parents to recognize more severe symptomatology which may require additional counseling (e.g., recurrent encopresis, persistent outbursts of anger, chronic hypervigilance).

Co-leaders add relevant comments during the session and support the leader. Most importantly, co-leaders give immediate support to students and parents who become emotionally distraught. They also help prevent disruption that may otherwise inhibit group dynamics. The title of the third role is doorkeeper. Persons performing this important role prevent nonparticipants from entering the session. Thus, news journalists and others not seeking treatment are prevented from speaking with participants during the debriefing experience. Doorkeepers also prevent severely distraught students or parents from bolting from sessions.

Before the Debriefing. Before the debriefing, team members should be apprised of the circumstances surrounding the debriefing. For example, is the debriefing the result of a death of a fellow student or teacher who died as a result of a terrorist act or due to the fact that children reside within the same city or near the site of a terrorist act? Or, is the debriefing in response to cumulative effects of terrorist activities? Additionally, teams should learn whether or not students' parents are at increased risk due to their occupations (e.g., fire fighters, law enforcement) or have a greater probability of being activated into military service (e.g., national guard, army reserves). These factors will likely have an influence upon participants' perceptions of terrorist acts and the moods with which the students and parents present.

Separate Debriefings for Parents and Students. Parent and student needs are often different and cannot be adequately addressed through a single session. Thus, the first session is conducted with parents. It is important to keep the number of parents in these sessions small (i.e., less than 12). Parents most often express frustration and anger regarding their inability to adequately protect their children from terrorism. Many will perceive the situation as "hopeless" and feel the events and dangers are "out of their control."

Thus, it is imperative that the team keep parents focused on the immediate needs of their children and not make promises related to future student safety. Such promises cannot be guaranteed and detract from the students' immediate reeds. Parents need to be continually reminded that the primary goals of this session are to: (a) educate parents regarding possible symptoms their children may exhibit, (b) offer available referral sources, and (c) remind parents regarding their role in validating their children (which is not the same as validating possibly unfounded child presented concerns) and normalizing their childrens' concerns.

Student survivors of terrorism often are responding to their own perceived needs and concerns. Younger children, especially, are emotionally vulnerable and look to parents and teachers to protect them. Often they require reassurances of safety and indications from parents that the crisis is over. Therefore, the team must encourage a sense of security and calmness during the joint student-parent session. Team members can foster this by slowing their speech rates and lowering their voice tones. Whenever possible, debriefings should occur in quiet rooms away from hallway and playground noise. Movable furniture comfortable for parents and children alike is helpful.

During this joint student-parent debriefing, two circles are formed. No more than five or six students of similar ages should sit in the inner circle with friends or familiar peers presenting with similar concerns. Parents should sit behind their children. This parental presence promotes a perception of stability, unity, and support, which can be heartening to students. An additional gesture of support can include parents placing their hands on their childrens' shoulders. This however should only occur when children are receptive to such gestures.

SEVEN ADAPTED FAMILY DEBRIEFING MODEL FOR SCHOOL STUDENTS STEPS

Introduction step. During the introduction step, the team leader identifies members of the team and establishes rules for the debriefing experience. Participants are asked to identify persons who may not belong in the room. Identified persons not directly related to the children or debriefing process are then asked to leave. Confidentiality and its limits are explained in terms understandable to the students and participants are encouraged not to discuss what is said within the session outside the debriefing room. All participants are encouraged to remain for the entire debriefing. The leader states that the primary purpose of the debriefing session is to help student survivors of terrorism better understand their feelings about the specific terrorist act, increase their coping skills related to continued terrorist threats, and gain increased levels of solace.

Fact gathering step. The second step of the process is fact gathering. Typically if the debriefing is related to a specific terrorist act that team members did not experience but students survivors did, the leader will begin by reporting that the team was not present during the terrorist act and asking children to report what the experience was like for students. Should the debriefing be related to recent terrorist acts which the students indirectly observed via media coverage rather than directly experienced, the leader may begin by asking about what the students saw on television. Those speaking are encouraged to give their name and state what they did when they first saw or heard about the terrorism. Emphasis is placed upon telling the facts of what each student saw or encountered, and team members do not push participants to describe their feelings about the incident. However, should students begin sharing feelings, the team leader and co-leaders should acknowledge emotions expressed and indicate that these feelings are normal.

Thought step. The third step is the thought step. This step is transitional and helps participants move from the cognitive domain to the affective domain. The leader asks questions related to what students thought when the terrorism erupted (e.g., "What was your first thought when you saw the airliner fly into the Twin Towers?"). During this step it is crucial to continue to validate and normalize each student's reported thoughts and perceptions.

Reaction step. The thought step can quickly give way to the emotionally charged reaction step. Here, the focus should be kept upon participants' sharing their reactions to the terrorism. Typically, the leader will start with a question like, "What has been the most difficult part of seeing the airliner fly into the Twin Towers?"

Symptom step. During the symptom step, the leader helps direct the group from the affective domain back to the cognitive domain. As emotionally charged reactions begin to subside, the leader uses age-appropriate language to ask students about any physical, cognitive, or affective symptoms experienced since the violent episode. For example, a leader might ask something like, "Have any of you felt kind of tingly in your tummies since you saw this on television?" Often the leader will discuss symptoms such as nausea, trembling hands, inability to concentrate, or feelings of anxiety. Typically, the leader will ask those who have encountered such experiences to raise their hands. Such a show of hands helps normalize the described symptoms and often helps survivors experience relief.

Teaching step. A teaching step follows the symptom step. Symptoms experienced by group members are reported in age-appropriate ways as being both normal and expected. Possible future symptoms can be briefly described (e.g., reoccurring dreams of being attacked, restricted range of affect). This helps both parents and students better understand symptoms that they may encounter in the future and gives permission to discuss such symptoms should they arise. During this teaching step the group leader may ask, "What little things have you done or noticed your friends, teachers, and parents doing that have helped you handle this situation so well?" This question suggests that the students are doing well and helps them begin to look for signs of progress rather than continuing to focus upon past or future terrorist episodes. Sometimes older students will express feelings of support from peers, teachers, or parents. Younger students may use active fantasy to help them better cope with their fears or concerns. An example of such active fantasy is a child pretending that he or she is a hero who disarms a terrorist and protects the other children from harm.

Re-entry step. The re-entry step attempts to place some closure on the experience and allows survivors and their parents to discuss further concerns or thoughts. The leader may ask students and parents to revisit pressing issues, discuss new topics or mention thoughts which might help the debriefing process come to a more successful end. After addressing any issues brought forward by the students or parents, the debriefing team makes a few closing comments related to any apparent group progress or visible group support. A hand-out written at an age-appropriate reading level for students and another written for adults discussing common reaction symptoms can be helpful. Younger children may prefer drawing faces which depict how they currently feel (e.g., anxious, sad, frightened). Later parents can use these pictures as conversation starters with their children at home. Hand-outs should list a 24-hour helpline number and include the work telephone number for the student's school counselor. Often, it is helpful to introduce parents to their child's school counselor at the debriefing.

POST-SESSION ACTIVITIES

After the session, team members should mingle with parents and children as refreshments are served. Team members should be looking for those who appear shaken or are experiencing severe distress. These persons should be encouraged to immediately meet with a counselor. The promotion of peer support (both parent and student) is important. Students and parents should be encouraged to telephone one another over the next few days to aid in the recovery process.

SUMMARY AND CONCLUSION

The described Adapted Family Debriefing Model for school students demonstrates promise for helping both student survivors of terrorism and their parents to cope with potentially negative residual psychological and social effects. The model has distinct differences from traditional CISD and was developed specifically for school-age students. The model is relatively easy to implement and can be readily modified to meet the specific needs of students and parents alike.

References

Juhnke, C. A. (1997). After school violence: An adapted critical incident stress debriefing model for student survivors and their parents. Elementary School Guidance & Counseling. 31, 163-170.

Mitchell, J. T., & Everly, C. S. (1993). Critical incident stress debriefing (CISD): An operations manual for the prevention of traumatic stress among emergency services and disaster workers, Ellicott City, MD: Chevron Press.

O'Hara, D. M., Taylor, R., & Simpson, K. (1994). Critical incident stress debriefing: Bereavement support in schools developing a role for an LEA education psychology service. Educational Psychology in Practice, 10, 27-33.

Thompson, R. (1990). Post-traumatic loss debriefing: Providing immediate support for survivors of suicide or sudden loss. Greensboro, NC: ERIC Clearinghouse on Counseling and Student Services. (ERIC Document Reproduction Services No. ED 315 708)

Gerald A. Juhnke, PhD, NCC, is Associate Professor of Education at The University of North Carolina at Greensboro.

Reprinted with permission from "Helping People Cope with Tragedy & Grief," published by ERIC Counseling and Student Services Clearinghouse.

Excerpted from "Will They Fly a Plane Into Our House"
Lawrence E. Shapiro

These are some of the questions that I have been asked over the last few days. If you need help in answering other questions, seek advice from a counselor at your child's school or from a community mental health agency.

Q. *What can I do to help keep my child from worrying about terrorism?* Most importantly, spend a lot of time with your child.

Other things that you can do include:
- Keep your child's schedule consistent.
- Know your community resources and use them if needed.
- Find your own help if you need it.
- Communicate.
- Openly express your affection to your child and those around you.
- Avoid arguing with your spouse.
- Do not use alcohol or drugs to make yourself feel better.
- Be truthful.
- Limit TV.
- Keep your child busy learning and doing productive activities.
- Foster a sense of tolerance and a sense of togetherness.
- Talk about what your child should do in an emergency.
- Find out what your school is doing.
- Find time for creative expression.
- Recognize your child's vulnerability to other problems.

Q. *What are some signs that my child is having trouble?*

Symptoms of anxiety disorders include:
- Recurring nightmares.
- Recurring thoughts.
- Extreme withdrawal, sadness, and a reluctance to do normal activities.
- Continued fearfulness when hearing about the trauma.
- Reluctance to go to school or to be away from parents.
- Extreme alertness, as if waiting for something bad to happen.

If you are concerned at all, seek professional guidance. Do not wait for symptoms to appear before you seek help.

Q. *My 8-year-old child doesn't seem to be affected at all by the terrorist attack even though it is constantly on television and everyone in the family is talking about it. Is this a problem?*

There are different reasons why a child may not want to deal with his feelings. You should not force your child to talk about his feelings, but you should make it clear that you have feelings about what has happened and you are available to talk when he is ready. Reading the questions and answers in Part II of this book and doing the activities in Part III may help.

Q. *My child says that he wants to join the army and kill all the terrorists. It's all he talks about. All he wants to do is play with his soldiers and 'kill the bad people.' Is that a bad thing?*

Children, particularly boys, often react to a perceived threat with bravado and heightened aggression in their play. This is an appropriate way for them to deal with their anxiety, as long as it is not the only way. Use the activities in this book to help your child express a range of feelings, find ways to help others, and develop a positive attitude.

Q. *We have a family vacation planned for Christmas. My child doesn't want to go because it means getting on a plane. Should we cancel the trip?*

This is your decision, not your child's decision. Many people are canceling planned flights. But other people feel that they cannot give in to fear and they must live their lives as normally as possible. When you have made the decision that is best for you and your family, explain your reasons simply and calmly to your child.

Q. *I know that I should be talking more to my child, but I'm too upset. I'm afraid that I'm going to break down in front of my child. Which is better: to keep silent or to fall apart?*

You have more choices than keeping silent or falling apart. I suggest that you read through Part II of this book by yourself and then see if some of it is appropriate to read with your child. The activities in Part III are not directly about terrorism, and might be a good way to open up communication with your child.

If you continue to feel too upset to talk to your child, then you should consider talking to a counselor about your own anxieties.

Q. *My child already had anxiety about a lot of things. He is afraid of dogs and escalators, to name just a few things, and he is very shy with strangers. Is this just going to make things worse?*

Children who already have worries and fears are more at risk when there is a traumatic event that affects them or those they love. Children who have excessive fears and anxieties benefit from counseling, and in particular, group counseling with children of the same age. Excessive shyness can become a serious and lifelong problem, but will respond to counseling. I would recommend contacting your school counselor or school psychologist to find out the resources that are available to you and your child.

Answers to Children's Questions

There are several principles to remember in talking to children about difficult topics:

- Keep your answers simple.
- Accept the fact that children may need to ask the same questions several times and need to have the same answers repeated to them.
- Tell the truth, even if it is upsetting. Children are much more resilient than most of us realize.
- Share your feelings, but do so in a calm and measured manner. Show children that all feelings are okay, but it is what you do with them that counts.
- Invite children to come to you with their questions and concerns at any time.
- Make sure that your voice, tone, and body language express your sincerity as well as your confidence.
- If you don't know an answer to a child's question, or if you don't feel that you can discuss it, then be honest about it. Don't try to fake it. Say, "That is a good question, and I need to think about a good answer. Let me talk to you about this later."

Answers to Children's Questions About Terrorists

Q. *What is a terrorist?*

Terrorists are people with a great deal of hate in their heart. They have so much hate that they want to harm and scare the people they hate, even though they don't know them.

Some people hate the United States because they think that our country has hurt them or their families. They will do anything they can to hurt us and scare us. They believe that they are at war with our country and that it is okay to hurt and kill people.

We know that this kind of thinking is very wrong. Some people may have reason to be angry or even to hate others, but violence is never a good answer.

Q. *Why are terrorists attacking our country?*

For many children in America, this is the first time you have heard about terrorists or what they can do. Unfortunately, this is not true in other countries. In Ireland, in some African countries, and particularly in the Middle East countries, terrorists have been trying to hurt people for many years.

You should know that children in these countries are often frightened. They see terrible things on TV and even in person. But even so they are children just like you and do things just like you.

They play, and go to school, and do things with their friends.

I cannot tell you exactly why terrorists attacked our country on September 11, 2001. As of today, we still don't even know who planned the attacks.

Sometimes terrorists tell you the reasons why they are attacking, and sometimes they do not. Part of the reason for a terrorist attack is always that they want to scare you. That is what the word "terror" means—that you are very, very afraid, like when you see a scary movie.

Q. *Are we in a war?*

Yes, the leaders of our country say that we are at war with terrorism and specially the people who hijacked the airplanes and attacked the World Trade Center and the Pentagon. But this is very different than other wars that America has fought. In other wars, we sent the Army, Navy, and Air Force to fight in other countries. But in this war, we are not even sure who is our enemy.

All our military forces are ready for war. Their first job will be to make sure that everyone in the United States and American citizens around the world are safe.

Q. *Will there be more terrorist attacks?*

This is one question that no one can really answer. However, I can tell you that there are thousands of people that are going to work to make this country safer and make sure that you and your family are safe. The President and the Congress have made this their #1 concern. The Army, the Navy, the Coast Guard, the Marines, the police, the firemen and firewomen, people who work in the airports, and many, many more people are going to do everything that they can to prevent anyone else from getting hurt.

Q. *Will they bomb my school or my home?*

Terrorists try to make you feel that you are not safe. Fear is their primary weapon. But if we look back at the history of terrorism around the world, terrorists rarely try to attack places where there are children. They are most likely to attack government buildings or military installations.

Today, people volunteer to go in the military. It is their choice. No one has to go if they don't want

to go, but many people feel that protecting our country is a very important job. In other wars, there was something called the "draft," and young men had to join the military unless they had health problems. It is not likely that we will have that kind of war again, where thousands of people are needed for the military, but it is possible. Even if this did happen, you would know many, many months before your dad or mom had to go into the military.

Q. *I am worried and I have trouble sleeping. What should I do?*

The first thing that you need to do is to talk to your parents. They need to know that you are worried. They may want you to see a counselor or someone else to help you talk about your feelings.

Here is trick that I sometimes teach children who are worried and have problems falling asleep. Maybe it will work for you.

While you are trying to fall asleep, think about your feet. Are your feet all right? Good. Now think about your legs. Are they okay? Good. Now think about your stomach, and then your chest, and your arms and your hands. Do they feel okay, too? Great. Now your shoulders. Now your neck. Now your head. Everything is okay. You just made sure that you are fine. Now you can go to sleep.

Q. *Is it safe to fly in an airplane?*

Air safety has always been a concern, just like car safety or bicycle safety. When something bad happens and people get hurt, we do things to make sure that this will never happen again. When I was young, we didn't have seat belts in cars. We didn't wear helmets when we rode our bicycles. Now we know better, and when you ride in a car or ride your bike you are safer than I was at your age. In the future, we will see many things change at airports and on airplanes that will make them even safer than they were before.

From: Shapiro, Lawrence E. (2001). Will They Fly a Plane into Our House? How to talk to children about terrorism. Norwalk, CT: Play2Grow. [ED454488] Full text available at: http://www.play2grow.com

Reprinted with permission from "Helping People Cope with Tragedy & Grief," published by ERIC Counseling and Student Services Clearinghouse.

Counseling Today, Laurie Hayes

For the first time in more than 100 years, a war is being fought, at least in part, on American soil. Terrorist attacks have turned city streets into the front lines and our country's private citizens are finding themselves threatened by a largely invisible enemy.

Thousands of civilians lost their lives in the first wave of violence on Sept. 11 when four hijacked jetliners crashed into the World Trade Center complex in New York City, the Pentagon building outside Washington, D.C., and a field near Pittsburgh. The victims of those attacks were apparently targeted for doing nothing more threatening than earning a living.

In sharp contrast to this very discernible destruction and tragic loss of life, a second, more insidious assault is currently underway in the form of bioterrorism, and once again those in harm's way are members of America's working class.

Mail laced with anthrax, a potentially deadly biological agent, began showing up at businesses and government offices in early October. While largely ineffective in terms of a physical toll—only a handful of those exposed to the chemical have succumbed to the disease —the emotional toll that the anthrax scare has exacted on the American public has been significant.

By midmonth, news organizations, including NBC, CBS and The New York Times, found themselves making headlines as well as reporting them, as letters containing white powder—some found to be anthrax, others harmless substitutes—arrived at their offices. To date, anthrax-tainted mail has also been delivered to numerous federal buildings, endangering both government workers and postal employees.

While conducting exhaustive investigations into the origin of the letters, government officials from President George W. Bush on down have been working to convince the American people that they are safe, emphasizing that the risk posed by anthrax is relatively low and that all of the appropriate precautions are being taken to guard against widespread infection.

But as political leaders have taken crash courses in microbiology in order to dispel people's fears, employers have also been put in a position of safeguarding their offices and reassuring their staffs, many of whom were already on edge following the Sept. 11 attacks.

The counselors and other mental health professionals who work with Employee Assistance Programs are playing a key role in this effort, according to Donald Jorgensen Jr., president of the Jorgensen Group, an EAP service and consulting firm in Tucson, Ariz.

"I know that in workplaces that have been targeted, either by the terrorist attacks or by anthrax, the EAPs have been quite active," Jorgensen said.

Jorgensen, who is president-elect of the Employee Assistance Professionals Association, stresses that EAPs deserve to be at the forefront of the response effort.

"Because most employee assistance professionals are trained to deal with traumatic events, they can deliver crucial critical incident stress debriefings," he said. Jorgensen emphasizes the importance of proper training in the area, adding, "I know of cases in which EAP professionals have been called in to repair the damage caused when such debriefings were not conducted appropriately."

This effort has been ongoing since Sept. 11. "There is no time limit on experiencing trauma," Jorgensen explains. "But fortunately there is also no time limit on helping those affected."

According to Jorgensen, utilization of EAP services "has easily increased by a factor of 10 or more" within organizations that are dealing firsthand with terrorist acts, such as the airlines, companies with employees at the site of the World Trade Center, the U.S. Postal Service and the media.

Because of their New York City location, Pat

Drew, director of the Life Skills/Employee Assistance Program at The New York Times, noted that her office had already been attending to the emotional needs of Times employees in the aftermath of the incident at the World Trade Center. So when a letter containing a suspicious white powder arrived at a third floor newsroom, her office, which consists of herself and two part-time counselors, responded with more of the same.

(Judith Miller, a reporter at The Times, opened the letter, which was postmarked from St. Petersburg, Fla., on Oct. 12. According to Toby Usnik, director of Public Relations, the newsroom was evacuated and Miller and approximately 30 other colleagues were tested for exposure and given the antibiotic Cipro. The New York City Department of Health found the culture negative for dangerous biological materials, including anthrax. Another envelope containing a white powdery substance was opened in the Times mailroom on Oct. 23. Similar procedures were followed, Usnik said. That powder also tested negative for anthrax.)

Drew, also a member of EAPA, described a three-pronged approach that was put into place after Sept. 11 and continues to be called into service as events unfold. The first step, she said, was the distribution of literature to all employees that gave tips for administering what she calls "emotional first-aid."

"The communication described how to take care of oneself and significant others in the aftermath of the attacks, as well as suggesting ways in which to talk to children about the incidents," she said. While admitting up front that "We have no pattern of behavior to draw upon that serves as an internal set of guidelines to follow, no emotional folder marked 'Terrorist Attack,'" the primer offered workers some ideas about how to help themselves and each other to get through the tragedy.

"It was very well received and seemed to be very helpful," Drew said.

The second prong of the EAP approach was conducting critical incident stress debriefings and other employee discussion groups, which, Drew noted, were attended by hundreds of Times employees.

"We invited employees to share what they had gone through and help them learn what to expect in terms of their own reactions," she said. "Research has shown that giving people an opportunity to talk about their experiences can be very healing. People start to think they might be crazy when they continue to be troubled by nightmares, flashbacks, etc., in the days and weeks following a traumatic incident. It helps to know that other people are dealing with the same thing."

"But we also stressed that no reaction was abnormal and that a person's response was very much dependant on previous traumas, personality and other factors," she added. "In addition, we tried to provide them with the resources they needed to move forward."

Families were also invited to take part in the debriefings and group meetings. This was crucial, according to Drew, who said the recent events have caused a lot of rethinking among families regarding their priorities.

The third phase of the EAP's approach involves identifying individuals or groups of employees who may require further assistance. The anthrax scares have made this effort all the more important, Drew said, because for people who were just starting to get their bearings back following the Sept. 11 attacks, the threat of a chemical assault was "another punch in the stomach."

To aid department heads in recognizing employees who could benefit from additional help, the EAP office distributed a briefing for managers, entitled "Managing Through the Upheaval from 9/11: A Guide for Helping Your People."

The document first congratulated the managers on the skill and sensitivity they had demonstrated to date — "They don't teach this stuff in journalism or business school," the briefing noted—and then offered some guidelines for further assisting their staffs.

In addition to describing situations in which referring employees to the EAP would be appropriate and even advisable, the guide advised managers to allow for a wide range of reactions among their staff, and stressed the importance of keeping employees updated on security measures and talking about what's going on, both at work and in the world.

Drew lauds the efforts of Times' management from the newsroom on up the corporate ladder for their efforts in that regard. She and Usnik stress that the paper's executives have done an excellent job in terms of leadership and communication.

"It's really been a team effort across all of the departments," Usnik said. "People want to know what's happening, and our senior management has been very forthcoming with answers."

He said this communication has come in face-to-face meetings, over the company's public address system or via e-mail and voicemail, depending on the circumstance.

"We have also been very concerned with consistency in the messages that go out to the employees, making sure that the company is speaking with one voice," Usnik added.

To date, the Times' EAP office has seen about two to three times the "normal" number of clients, and Drew expects that this will be the case for the foreseeable future. "We are looking at this in terms of a marathon, as opposed to just a series of sprints," she said.

Jorgensen, of EAPA, supports this approach, especially in light of the upcoming holiday season.

"The holidays, with the potential for increased travel as well as an additional focus on mail services, will likely add to employees' stress levels," he said. This will be the case, he said, whether or not they believe that their workplace could be a terrorist target.

"In reality," Jorgensen acknowledges, "it is really very difficult to find folks who have not been affected in some way by the terrorist actions. I believe that EAPs are experiencing an increased workload across the board."

And this is not likely to change anytime soon, he said. In fact, Jorgensen believes that EAP professionals need to work to be even more visible and solidify their role in crisis response and management.

As their responsibilities increase, Roger Lambert, president of the National Career Development Association, a division of the American Counseling Association, noted that it is important to remember that EAP providers may also require assistance in dealing with their work experiences.

"These counselors are in the position to help people who have found themselves in terrible situations," Lambert said. "But they need to avoid getting too involved with their clients and understand that they can't absorb all of their problems.

"Like the firefighters who are responding at the scene, counselors can only handle so much," he cautioned. "They need to make a conscious effort to focus on other things when they are off the job, such as doing things with their kids, tending a garden or other types of activities that are more 'normal.'"

Drew reiterates the importance of counselors taking the time to process their own feelings. "There is such a drive to do the right thing and to help as much as possible that it is very easy to lose site of the importance of self-care," she said. "But we have to set limits on the amount of work we can do or we will become victims ourselves."

In fact, good advice for all involved in the aftermath of Sept. 11 is contained in the guidelines Drew prepared for her New York Times management team:

"Remember, what makes this so tough is that we are all, to varying degrees, going through this. If you are trying to get through this without stopping to take care of yourself, just cut it out. Call us, call other managers, visit with your people and acknowledge that you've been struggling with this as well. Being stoic and managerial sends the wrong message. Being human and having feelings sends the right one."

This article originally appeared in ACA's Counseling Today, *December, 2001.*

How Should HR and Managers React in the Aftermath of Terrorism Events?

John Sullivan

Although recent terrorist events may have occurred thousands of miles away from you, there are many potential people-related problems that may still occur at your location. Strategic HR people need to react quickly to business problems and managers need to realize that uncertainty and inaction can actually increase anxiety, so clearing the air and stating a company's plan of action (in response to terrorism events) is an essential first step.

Although HR professionals and managers can't prevent all of the potential problems that traumatic events like this can cause, it is important that they should at least be aware of them and have a plan of action.

Potential Employee Fears and Anxiety

1. Employees may fear working in (or even near) tall buildings, especially landmark or symbolic buildings.
2. Employees will likely fear taking commercial airline flights, especially out of major airports. Some may even refuse to fly.
3. Employees in the New York and Washington areas and all airline and financial services employees are likely to have friends or coworkers that suffered directly as a result of the traumatic events. Expect any anxiety related to losing friends to last for at least several days. Employees in other major cities are also likely to suffer from a general malaise and anxiety as a result of the extensive and graphic news coverage.

Employee Relations Issues

1. Expect an overall decrease in productivity, an increase in hallway conversations and a desire to listen to the news.
2. Employees perceived as being from certain ethnic and religious groups are likely to fear retaliation and or blame from either customers or co-workers.
3. Some employees or customers may actually begin to harass any employees perceived as being from certain ethnic and religious groups.
4. Expect increased absenteeism/late arrivals and increased vacation requests during this period.
5. Expect employees stranded as a result of flight cancellations to be anxious.
6. Expect your international employees to have increased fears of terrorism and air travel.
7. If you have people missing or dead from the doomed flights or who were in buildings that were damaged, anticipate the need for grief counseling and immediate financial support. Talk to your legal staff about any potential legal or insurance liabilities.
8. Expect a slowdown in recruiting and turnover because few people will be moving/looking during this uncertain period.

Possible Solutions: Things a Manager Can Do

1. Keeping people busy and getting them back to work is important because it keeps their minds off of current events. Urge employees to come to work and to get back into their routine immediately, wherever possible.
2. Educate managers about the possible anxiety problems and employee concerns. Suggest tools or approaches they should use. Urge managers to talk directly to their employees about these issues and respond rapidly to their requests.
3. Designate an HR person to be the primary contact for issues related to this event.
4. Provide onsite or telephone counseling for anxiety.

5. Add an information section to your website which covers issues related to this event.

6. If individual workers are clearly being disruptive (because of their anxiety) send them to counseling or home.

7. Contact your employees in international locations that might be at risk for terrorism or retaliation. Ask them what they need and respond rapidly to the requests.

8. Allow or even encourage workers to take time off to work for charities or to give blood, in order to meet their need to "do something" to help.

9. Encourage employees who see harassment (of employees perceived to be from certain religious and ethnic groups) to report it immediately. Remind employees of the penalties for harassment. Assign an HR professional to handle these cases and identify any employees that may be "at risk" of violence or harassment.

10. Be more flexible in requests for using sick leave and vacation for the next week.

11. Allow workers time to call friends and relatives and to talk out their concerns.

12. Allow stressed workers to work at home or to use sick days until their anxieties subside.

13. Allow workers to postpone or cancel immediate business trips that require commercial flights.

14. Involve the workers (or union) in the process of alleviating anxiety in order to lessen their fears and to get their "ownership" of the problem.

15. Tell employees that you will keep them informed about any new events through emails or the loudspeaker, so they have no need to constantly listen to the "news."

16. Cancel or postpone upcoming conferences or events that may require a large number of people to fly commercial carriers (especially to New York or Washington).

17. Contact your employee assistance program vendor to see what services they offer and if they are gearing up for the extra counseling that will be needed.

18. If you have people missing or possibly even dead (that were on the flights or who were in the New York and Washington area's that were damaged) be prepared to offer immediate financial and counseling support to the families.

19. Take this is an opportunity to review and upgrade your disaster plan.

Dr. John Sullivan (JohnS@sfsu.edu) is professor and head of the HR program at San Francisco State University. More employment related articles can be found at www.drjohnsullivan.com.

Reprinted with permission. The article originally appeared on the Electronic Recruiting Exchange, www. erexchange.com.

DON'T LET TERRORISM SUCCEED: GET BACK TO WORK! 16

John Sullivan

It might seem insensitive, given the recent tragic deaths in New York and Washington, but it's not. If you take a step back and think about it, in a time of war we all need to act like "Rosie the Riveter" and get back to work in order to rebuild the economy.

They Declared War on Our Economy — It's Economic Terrorism

Let there be no doubt in anyone's mind: it's no accident that the prime target of the terrorist attack was both the symbolic and actual center of the financial economy of the United States. As citizens, employees, and managers we can't be naïve. Realize that no terrorists group is strong enough to hurt us militarily. They wouldn't even try. The terrorists specifically targeted the Wall Street area and the World Trade Center, not just with the goal of destroying buildings, but with a much more dastardly objective: to kill our financial leaders and to disrupt our economy and financial markets.

The Goal of the Terrorist: "It's the Economy Stupid"

We are the business and economic leader of world. We are the symbols of successful capitalism. Those that wish to harm us could have killed many more people by crashing into a packed sports stadium. Instead, with deliberate intent, they struck at the heart of our economy. To put it bluntly, the terrorists sought to kill our financial leaders and to distract and disrupt the thousands of hardworking individuals that run our financial markets. They struck with the intent to crush consumer confidence and to drive us into recession, because that is where terrorism can have the biggest impact, if we let it!

What Can You Do?

Although recent terrorist events may have occurred thousands of miles away from where you work, you need to realize that the terrorists were aiming directly at you and your wallet.

Each of us can't rebuild the World Trade Center brick by brick. However there are many things individuals, employees, managers, customers, and consumers can do to help us win this war against our economy. What can you do to thwart the undermining of our financial institutions and our economy? Start with these nine steps.

Nine Economic Weapons for Defeating Terrorism

1. *Time for mourning.* Yes, we need time to mourn our dead. Individual managers and corporations can do their part by allowing us the time and the flexibility we need to get over our hurt and anxiety. Managers can use this catastrophe as an opportunity to show they care by asking workers individually what they need to get over their anxiety and then providing it to the point where it exceeds their expectations. As individual employees, we must be strong and rapidly get back to work, because the longer we delay, the greater the terrorist victory.

2. *Work smarter.* As individual employees, we also need to work harder and smarter in order to increase our productivity. By doing so we send an immediate message to the terrorists. That message is, you can kill thousands of our citizens but the remaining employees, union members, government workers, and managers will respond by working together and increasing our nation's output to beyond what it was before you struck.

3. *Be confident.* As consumers we were targets, not directly from an airplane crash, but indirectly through the loss of our confidence in the economy. We can't let the terrorists win. Instead as consumers, we must act as soldiers in the economic war. We need to remain confident in our economic and financial institutions. We need to keep spending and to urge others to spend wisely. In addition, we need to plan for the future, buy American, talk up the economy, and remain optimistic.

4. *Keep traveling.* One way terrorists expect to stifle our economy is by slowing our transportation system through the delays caused by increased security and an increased fear of flying. But we need to be strong and to continue to travel. We must meet any delays we encounter with a smile. Individuals need to overcome their fears of flying and keep commerce moving. We need to show our support for the airline industry in general and for the employees of United Airlines and American Airlines specifically, who have suffered through great personal adversity. They lost many friends and colleagues, but they also got back to work and kept on flying.

5. *Buy stock.* The terrorists aimed their flying bomb at Wall Street to depress our stock and bond markets. Our natural reaction during these times of uncertainty is to be cautious. But that only works in the terrorist's favor. Instead, we as consumers and fund managers need to be confident and increase our purchase of stocks and bonds in order to immediately build the stock market back to a level higher than where it was last week, before the terrorists hit.

6. *Buy from the targeted firms.* Both companies and consumers need to come to the aid of firms that were targeted as tenants of the World Trade Center. Corporate purchasing managers and consumers need to go out of their way in order to do business with these "damaged" firms so they can get quickly back on their feet. If you are already one of their customers, you need to be tolerant and understanding, because it will take them a little while to get back on their feet. If you are not a customer of these targeted firms, become one. Buy their products and services and recommend them to others.

7. *Visit New York and Washington D.C.* The terrorists had as part of their intent the weakening of the economies of our great cities. Terrorists want you to cancel business and tourist trips. They want companies to cancel conventions and conferences. But don't let the bad guys win. Find a way to visit these great cities in order to build their economies and make them strong again. If you can't visit, encourage friends to and instead buy products made in these great cities.

8. *Cooperate and help out.* If you are a competitor to one of the targeted firms, take a step back and give them a break for a short period. Instead of competing, cooperate and help them rebuild by lending them office space and equipment. Provide them with advice and resources. Help them by saying positive things about them to your colleagues and customers. Become a "cooperative competitor." Once they're back on their feet you can begin competing again.

9. *Don't buy from the enemy.* When the perpetrators are identified, let's hit them with our economic punch as well as our military punch. Refuse to buy products from and to travel to countries that harbor terrorists. Encourage your friends and neighbors to do the same. On the positive side, support the nations that cooperate in fighting the terrorist with your dollars.

What Does This All Mean?

We can't let the terrorist deal us a crushing economic blow. As individuals we must be strong. And even though our natural reaction is to be anxious as a result of this catastrophe, we need to do the exact opposite. As employees we need to work harder, work smarter and cooperate with our managers for the common good. As consumers we need to be optimistic and spent wisely.

That there be no doubt that the target of the terrorist was the economy. They didn't attack a military base. Instead, they attacked the very foundation of our financial system, in order to cripple our economic way of life. We must recognize this new enemy and its real target. Then we must respond just like "Rosie the Riveter" did during World War II. We need to get back to work...and the time is now!

Dr. John Sullivan (JohnS@sfsu.edu) is professor and head of the HR program at San Francisco State University. More employment related articles can be found at www.drjohnsullivan.com.
Originally published via the Electronic Recruiting Exchange (www.erexchange.com) on September 17, 2001 Reprinted with permission.

National Mental Health Association

In the aftermath of the terrorist attacks, and ongoing war, our world has drastically changed, and focusing on business-as-usual continues to be difficult. But returning to productive work is a necessary step in our healing, as individuals and as a nation.

The National Mental Health Association (NMHA) offers the following information to assist employers in responding to tragic events with the goal of helping them help their employees recover and return to productive life. We must remember, however, that for some people the effects of the disaster may not be felt immediately, but instead may arise in months and, in some cases, years to come.

SIGNS OF EMOTIONAL IMPACT

Over the coming months, employers may begin to see the emotional impact of the terrorist attacks in their workforce. This may play out in employees' performance and productivity in the following ways:

- Working slowly
- Missing deadlines
- Calling in sick frequently
- Absenteeism
- Irritability and anger
- Difficulty concentrating and making decisions
- Appearing numb or emotionless
- Withdrawal from work activity
- Overworking
- Forgetting directives, procedures and requests
- Difficulty with work transitions or changes in routines

WHAT EMPLOYERS CAN DO

To help your employees work through the emotional toll of the terrorist attacks and reduce the impact on your organization's productivity, NMHA recommends taking the following steps:

1. Speak to the entire organization as soon as possible. Leadership should meet with staff at all levels to express shared grief, as well as to promote available counseling services and other resources. Use the key messages included to plan your discussion.

2. Educate your supervisors and managers: Inform all supervisors and human resources professionals about the signs of emotional distress; all policy changes and actions being taken in response to the crisis; and available treatment resources so they can inform their staff. Direct them to encourage staff to seek treatment when necessary. Most importantly, remind them that they should seek support as needed, in addition to facilitating this for the people they supervise.

3. Provide educational resources: Your employee assistance program (EAP) and/or mental health administrator may have educational materials and information on covered treatment resources. NMHA has resources available on coping with loss, helping children cope, post-traumatic stress disorder and other topics through its Web site (www.nmha.org) and toll-free number (800-969-NMHA).

4. Facilitate communication among employees: Support among colleagues can help employees work through difficulties. Consider allowing people to break from work periodically to talk. Provide a comfortable environment for them to gather.

5. Consider bringing a professional counselor/facilitator on-site: A professional, or multiple professionals, can conduct group meetings and provide individual counseling. Such an approach can help you identify and get help to those who need it, which will alleviate their immediate

pain and reduce their need for services down the road.

6. Revamp your leave policy temporarily: Allow people time off beyond the norm for donating blood, community activity and personal needs. Employees will benefit significantly from feeling that they are able to take positive action and make a difference.

7. Reconsider your current travel needs: Employees, clients and other individuals may be hesitant to make business trips for some time. Consider postponing or canceling upcoming conferences and other meetings that require travel. Your EAP may assist staff in dealing with flight anxiety. You also may need to revamp your travel policy as flight security regulations change.

8. Organize community action: Hold a blood drive at your worksite, collect clothes and food for the victims and their families, or start a voluntary collection fund for relief efforts. Show employees that your organization is committed to helping those in the workplace, as well as the community at large.

9. Plan for future emergencies: Create or review your organization's emergency plan to address any situations that arose with the recent disaster. Make sure to involve all segments of your staff in the planning.

KEY MESSAGES FOR YOUR STAFF

Talking with staff at a difficult time like this can feel like a daunting task. Below are some suggested key messages that may help you communicate with your employees and facilitate their recovery and return to productive work.

- We grieve. Find out if any employees have lost family, friends or acquaintances. Share your grief and offer support.
- Know what to expect of yourself. You may experience emotions of denial, disbelief, confusion, shock, sadness, yearning, anger, humiliation, despair and guilt, and you may not be prepared for the intensity and duration of your emotions or how swiftly your moods may change. However, these feelings are common, healthy and will help you come to terms with this tragedy. Be aware that you may resolve your feelings and symptoms but then have a recurrence of traumatic symptoms during stressful times, such as retirement, divorce, or loss of a loved one.

- Talk and listen patiently with your co-workers. If you feel grief, anxiety or anger, you are not alone. Talk to your colleagues who are experiencing the same feelings. Some may have gone through the aftermath of other disasters. When listening, don't try to "fix it" or offer false comfort, especially if somebody has lost a loved one. Instead, offer a simple expression of sorrow and take time to listen to them. Where possible, offer to help them with tasks of daily life, such as errands, cooking and shopping. Discourage damaging ways of coping such as excessive drinking. Don't hesitate to recommend professional help when you feel someone is experiencing too much pain to cope alone.

- Be aware that people will respond differently and recover at different paces. Some will want to get back to work to regain a sense of control, and others will have difficulty focusing for some time. This is a normal response to a crisis. Many people survive disasters without developing significant psychological problems, but many may need assistance.

- Business will go on. Acknowledge that work will be subdued and perhaps very different in some ways, depending on your particular industry and how severely it was impacted, but there will be continuity. Returning to productive work will help with healing as individuals and as a nation.

- Many people with family in the government, military, or living oversees may be concerned for their ongoing safety. Ask employees if they fall into this category, and encourage them to seek support and care as needed.

- Many employees who are required to travel for work may be afraid to do so. Reassure them that this is a normal reaction, and that you have their safety in mind first and foremost. Tell them about any short-term travel policy changes, and let them know they will be revamped as necessary as more information becomes available from the government and the airlines.

- While anger is a natural reaction, prejudice and racism will not be tolerated. It was hatred that caused these senseless and despicable events, and we must not permit ourselves to sink to that level by expressing hostility to members of specific ethnic and religious groups in the workplace, among our customers or in our communities.

(Staff who "look" Middle Eastern, have accents or are foreign nationals are potential objects of this prejudice.) Supervisors will challenge discriminatory remarks or actions, or any environment of harassment, and disciplinary action will be taken.

- Take care of yourselves and your families. Eat well, get plenty of rest and exercise, spend time with those closest to you, postpone major life decisions and other significant stressors when you can, and seek outside help when necessary.

- Take care of your children. Many of you who have children are concerned about their well being while you are at work and at home. There are several steps you can take to help them handle the effects of this crisis:
  - Turn off the TV when they are in the room;
  - Let them express their feelings and ask questions;
  - Share your own coping strategies with them;
  - Get back to your family routine as soon as possible; and
  - Reassure them that they are safe.

- Seek help if you need to. If your feelings are too much to bear, seeking help is a sign of strength, not weakness. Mental health problems—in general and in response to this tragedy—are real, diagnosable and treatable. People should not be embarrassed to seek the help that they need. Furthermore, mental health treatment (including both talk therapy and possibly medication) is very effective. The information you provide will vary depending upon your organization's resources, but may include information about your EAP, health plan, mental health administrator, and community resources. Make sure you have current provider listings available, as well as documents detailing available benefits and the processes for accessing care. Tell them whom to contact in your organization if they have trouble with accessing services or with the quality of care that they receive. Be aware that people with a history of trauma or mental health problems are more likely to have mental health treatment needs—as are those who have lost loved ones.

- Contact us with any concerns or suggestions. Let them know that the doors of your organization's leadership are open to them during this and other times of crisis. Designate a human resources or other manager as a contact person.

The National Mental Health Association has several resources available to help you and others cope, including Time for Reassurance, Talking with Kids, Coping Tips for Adults and fact sheets on post-traumatic stress, depression, coping with loss and other topics. To obtain this information, go to www.nmha.org or call our toll-free line 800-969-NMHA (6642).

Reprinted by permission. Copyrighted and published by National Mental Health Association. No part of this document may be reproduced without written consent.

Section Three

Shootings and Other Tragedies in the Schools

Columbine High School Three Years Later: Lessons Learned, Perspectives Gained

18

Betty Fitzpatrick

The worst school shooting in recent history took place on April 20, 1999 at Columbine High School in Jefferson County, Colorado. The facts are now part of history, but Eric Harris and Dylan Klebold killed 12 students, 1 teacher, wounded 24 others before killing themselves. While this was not the first school shooting (first recorded one was in 1927 in Bath, Michigan where a school board member killed 45 people including 38 students), it is the one that woke up the United States to the reality of school place violence.

Since that time, schools have become more aware of the need to plan for potential disasters that could directly affect schools. Our new reality demonstrates that schools need to plan for the possibility of natural disasters, man-made disasters, terrorists attacks and bio chemical disasters. The issue is not if this will happen, but when will it happen.

Is your school really safe?

The following pages will cover what one school district has done after a school shooting to prepare for any eventuality. Covered are specific challenges after a school shooting, broad range planning and emergency preparedness to include Threat Assessment, and community collaboration recommendations necessary to offer comprehensive support to schools.

Lessons Learned

1. **It is a marathon, not a sprint**
   Any school that experiences a violent act or major disaster, must be prepared to respond for the long term. Long-term effects, although different from immediate needs, are still significant, and will require additional support.

2. **The ripple effect**
   While it is easy to identify the direct victims, one must realize that survivors, families of victims, observers, staff, responders, community at large, and people who watched news coverage are all at risk for traumatization. In the first 10 days after the shootings, 3,000 hours of mental health services were delivered. (1)

3. **Community collaboration**
   The needs are enormous and schools are not designed or staffed to be the sole support to victims after a disaster. It is imperative that schools have partnerships with community agencies such as Mental Health, Red Cross, Law Enforcement, Emergency Medical Services, Fire Departments, Offices of Emergency Management, Public Health Departments, Salvation Army. The time to forge these partnerships is before the disaster hits, not after.

4. **Emergency plan for schools**
   Emergency Plans for schools are much more comprehensive than ever before. They should include emergency management plans, disaster preparedness, immediate crisis response, plans for returning to school and long-term support in the school setting for victims. The Emergency Plan should be a dynamic document. It should be reviewed periodically to include new issues. For example, does your plan include topics like biological terrorism or chemical and hazardous disasters?

5. **Appropriate training for mental health school staff**
   The instructional, academic model of schools does not always lend itself to the increased mental health needs of students. Does your mental health staff (including counselors, psychologist, social workers, nurses, behavioral specialists or other support staff)

have appropriate training for immediate crisis response? While Jefferson County School mental health staff had training for single incident crisis, we were not prepared to respond to multiple victims. Immediate training was necessary. Within 72 hours we offered training to our staff. There are many models available: NOVA, CISD, Sanford Model, Red Cross, or any variety of the above. The immediate psychological first aid should ensure that a sense of safety and security is reestablished.

It should provide:
a) An opportunity to talk about the personal experiences
b) Education for victims as to what to expect in their normal reactions to disasters and emotional trauma
c) Assistance in planning for necessary coping skills and support in the immediacy of the event
d) Re-establishment of normal routines

It is important to note that Crisis Response is not therapy. Therapy may be a necessary support in the long term, and appropriate referrals by qualified personnel should be made. Crisis Response seeks to restore and enhance adaptive capabilities.

6. Communications

School districts must work with their Public Information Officer (or community media person) to plan for responding in the event of a major disaster. A calm, articulate spokesperson should be available for frequent updates of information. Accurate and timely updates are critical, both internally and externally. Talking points should be developed. Strategies should be developed so school districts can competently handle local and national journalists. Know what can and cannot be discussed!

CHALLENGES TO SCHOOL CHILDREN AFTER VIOLENT ACTS

We are entering a new era; violence is becoming a more common occurrence in the lives of the school-age child. Although the Justice Policy Institute in Washington, DC, reported a decrease in the incidence of school-associated violent deaths, the National School Boards Association (NSBA) reports there are 3 million incidents of violence a year on campuses. These numbers have huge implications for schools that are constantly challenged by their leadership and communities to show increased academic success. The reality is that

children who are victims of or witnessed violence will have their cognitive abilities impaired—if not permanently, certainly temporarily.

A recent study by Dr. Hallum Hurt of the Albert Einstein Medical Center found that children who have witnessed violence exhibited more depression and anxiety than children with lower exposure. This led to a higher likelihood of missed school, poor grades, and emotional problems. Dr. Hurt also found that a majority of caregivers do not recognize the effects of violence on children.

While "official" surveys have not been conducted at Columbine High School, our experience has shown that significant numbers of students needed additional academic and emotional support immediately after the shootings and in the ensuing years. Support for students included Homebound Instruction, peer monitoring, private tutoring, increased group counseling and one on one therapy, shorter periods of instruction, etc. The challenge continues and we have no data on how the graduates have fared in the higher education arenas.

The number of victims of trauma and terror after the September 11th terrorist acts is in the hundreds of thousands. From the children who lost parents, relatives, or friends to the number of children who witnessed the event both directly or indirectly, there will be a huge impact on the educational systems, not only in New York City and Washington, DC, but across the country.

PROFILES OF SHOOTERS AND THREAT ASSESMENT

There were many attempts to profile a school shooter after the Columbine shootings. Both the FBI and Secret Service have released documents on school shooters. Both came to the same conclusion: there is no such thing as a profile of a school shooter. There are some commonalties among school shooters, but profiling can stereotype innocent students and create false positives. It creates bias against students who are different and may also exclude students who do not fit the profile but pose a risk of violence. Instead, schools should have a process of identification, support and referral for students who may be at risk of hurting themselves or others. There are several models listed in the Bibliography at the end of this chapter.

All include behavioral and warning signs as well as a process to identify degree of risk. The process should include:

- Referral
- Investigation
- Assessment model (include student, family, school and social information)
- Rate level of threat assessment (low, medium, high)
- Evaluation and response
- Referral to law enforcement/mental health

EMERGENCY PLANS FOR SCHOOL DISTRICTS SHOULD:

- Be comprehensive
- Have a building and district emergency response team
- Include annual training, with table top exercises and field exercises
- Be reviewed periodically
- Have a Crisis Response Team as an integral part of the team
- Be developed in partnership with local law enforcement, fire, EMS, Emergency Preparedness Office, Public Health and Mental Health
- Be communicated to staff, students, parents and the local community
- Include a "Go Box" for every school
- Minimize opportunities for serious injury, death and/or property damage
- Return school to normalcy as soon as possible

GO BOXES

Go Boxes are practical and necessary items for every school. They should include:

- Current demographics on students and staff
- Significant health problems list for students and staff
- Medication list for students and staff
- Blueprints of school building (to include utility shut off)
- Emergency evacuation plan for disabled students
- Walkie talkies/ cellular phones
- Yearbook/photos
- Emergency plan/crisis plan with important phone numbers

JEFFERSON COUNTY SCHOOLS EMERGENCY MANAGEMENT PLAN

The Emergency Management Plan for Jefferson County Schools is a comprehensive plan built on the Incident Command System. The Incident Command System (ICS) lends itself to one leader/decision maker, common organizational structures, common terminology, common operating procedures, reasonable span of control and transition of authority and responsibility. Roles and responsibilities include incident commander (IC), public information officer (PIO), liaison officer, operations chief, documentation and logistics.

The Emergency Plan includes a complete training manual and a quick reference flip chart for immediate use. The flip chart addresses natural and man made disasters to include:

- Biological terrorism
- Blizzard/snow conditions
- Bomb threat
- Building explosion
- Bus accidents
- Chemical threats
- Civil disturbance
- Drive by shooting
- Earthquake
- Fire
- Floods
- Food poisonings
- Hazardous materials
- Kidnapping/missing person
- Lightning
- Power lines down/utility failure
- School violence
- Sever winds/hail/thunderstorms
- Sexual assault
- Student/staff illness, injury, death
- Suicide
- Tornado

It also includes support—recovery, incident command system procedures, roles and responsibilities, key decisions to be made and resources and referral.

Copies of the Jefferson County Plan are available (fee charged): Jefferson County Schools, 1829 Denver West Dr., Golden, CO 80401, ATTN: Area Administrator (303) 982-6939.

CONCLUSION

Initially, after the Columbine shooting there was tremendous demand for counseling services. The school district was not able to meet the demand on its own. Partnerships were formed with our community mental health provider, University of Colorado Health Sciences Center, Department of Psychiatry, Red Cross,

Victims Assistance offices, the faith community—priests and pastors—and private providers.

Thousands of hours of services were provided. As we approached the beginning of the next school year after the shootings, additional school-based services were created through a variety of grants. Again, the need was great, although somewhat diminished from the immediate event.

An outside facility, Columbine Connections, was created so families, staff, and community members could access services outside the school building. In year two and now in year three, additional services continue, but at a reduced level, as demand has lessened. Other structures of support such as churches and private therapists seem better able to meet the need now.

At the conclusion of the 2002 school year, all extra funding will be depleted. Therefore, no additional positions at the school will be added and Columbine Connections will close its doors. This is not done without concern—but additional funding is no longer available. The school district will continue to monitor the situation. The desire, of course, would be to continue the extra support.

Bibliography

(1) Jefferson Center for Mental Health; Report on Services to Columbine. October, 2000.

(2) FBI: www.fbi.gov. *The School Shooter, A Threat Assessment*
SS: www.treas.gov/usss/NEA: *Early Warning Timely Response, A Guide to Safe Schools*, 1998.
http://www.ed.gov/offices/OSERS/OSEP/earlywrn.html.

Useful Websites
Josephson Institute
www.josephson institute.org

National Education Association
www.nea.org

American Counseling Association
www.counseling.org

National Institute for Mental Health
www.nimh.nih.gov

National Association of School Psychologists
www.nasponline.org

National Council for Social Studies
www.socialstudies.org

National Association of Elementary School Principals
www.naesp.org

National Association of Secondary School Principals
www.nassp.org

Jefferson County Schools
www.jeffco.k12.co.us

US Department of Justice
www.usdoj.gov

Betty Fitzpatrick, RN, MS, Director, Health Services, Jefferson County Schools, Colorado, was responsible for coordinating the school district crisis response to the Columbine shootings.

CRISIS IN THE SUMMER: THE TRAGEDY THAT LED TO "MEGAN'S LAW"

19

Maureen M. Underwood and Linda Powner

Hamilton Township is a small community in the west central part of New Jersey. Despite its proximity to Trenton, the capitol, the community is suburban in character, with residents connected across neighborhoods through school athletic teams, youth groups and church activities. Around dinnertime on Friday, July 29, 1994, word spread quickly through the community over police scanners that seven-year-old Megan K. had been reported missing. The neighborhood firehouse became the hub of search activities as groups of townspeople were organized into teams that canvassed streets and backyards looking for the child. Hope that Megan would be found alive ran high even as the search continued through the night and into early evening of the following day, when it was abruptly called off. One of the child's neighbors, a paroled sex offender, had admitted kidnapping the girl and murdering her in the house where he lived, across the street from the K. family. He took police to Megan's body, which he left on the ground near a soccer field.

THE RESPONSE STRATEGY

The guidance counselor at Megan's elementary school, who is a township resident, began her involvement as soon as she learned that the child was missing. She offered to be available at the firehouse during the search in the event Megan's friends wanted to talk with someone with whom they were familiar at school. The counselor also tried to contact the building principal and district superintendent to inform them of what had happened, but both were away for the weekend. Finally, she reached the Director of Guidance and Counseling, who was leaving on vacation the following day. He immediately went to his office to retrieve the district's policy for responding to sudden loss, and dropped it off at the counselor's home late that Saturday evening. He offered to cancel his vacation to

help with the response strategy, but as they reviewed the policy, which had been written for when school was in session, it appeared to provide enough specific guidelines to direct the school during summer recess and the counselor felt she could organize enough support to manage the crisis without requiring him to change his plans.

On Sunday morning, the counselor contacted the school secretary, who knew Megan's family personally. They arranged to go together to the K. home to offer condolences and to let the family know of the school's availability to address the emotional needs of Megan's two siblings who also attend district schools. The counselor continued to be accessible to the family in the days after the crisis, especially during the visitation and funeral.

Because this type of crime attracts a great deal of attention, the media was now camped out on the family's driveway, attempting to take pictures of anyone who entered or left the home. Their presence compounded the tension, fear, and sorrow that gripped the community. The circumstances of Megan's death had become national news and the grief of the family and community were no longer private. Neighbors had begun to distribute pink bows in memory of Megan (pink had been the child's favorite color). Within hours, these reminders of the tragedy were everywhere. There was virtually no way to escape or ignore the trauma, and that made the need to formalize a plan to meet the needs of the township's children even more critical.

Sunday afternoon the counselor began to construct a community support team by reaching out to other resources for help. She began by contacting clergy from all denominations to prepare them for the requests they might receive from families for guidance or support. Through these contacts, she compiled a list of clergy with specific training in grief counseling or pastoral counseling in the event she received requests at the school for such services. The local mental health agencies were also put on alert to anticipate referrals related to the crisis. Several of these agencies reported they had already been receiving calls and they offered to provide additional assistance to the school if it was needed. The counselor also contacted other guidance counselors and child study team members from the district to establish a team to be available for crisis counseling at the school the following day. Late Sunday night the counselor finally got in touch with the principal who had just returned to town. She informed him of the skeleton plan that had been put into place. He endorsed it and they arranged a meeting early Monday morning to continue to strategize.

On Monday, the superintendent and assistant superintendent returned to the district and met with the counselor and principal. They reviewed what the counselor had done up to this point in time and gave administrative support and approval. The superintendent suggested that a meeting be arranged as soon as possible with one of the special crisis consultants available through the State Department of Education to review the district's plans since the magnitude of the crisis seemed to be growing. Media attention had increased, pink bows were everywhere, and a rally was scheduled to be held in a local park on Tuesday with the New Jersey governor in attendance. In the interim, it was decided that the school would remain open and crisis stations would be set up where parents and children could meet with counselors who could provide support, discuss children's reactions, and suggest helpful strategies for parental response. Megan's classroom teacher would also be available at the school to offer a reassuring presence to the children who were closest to Megan.

Because of the nature of the event, the community was charged with fear and outrage, so the crisis counselors were provided with resource materials to help them deal more effectively with the reactions that might be anticipated after the homicide of a young child. A letter was sent out to all school parents through the principal's office to notify them that the school would be open to provide counseling for children, and to assist parents in making decisions about their children during this crisis. Counselors were especially prepared to talk with parents about their children's attendance at Megan's wake and funeral. At the same time, the counselor requested that the local library assemble a collection of resource materials on grief and bereavement. These were organized in a special section of the library and placed in reserve. Hospice

was also contacted; they supplied additional resource materials on grief, which were duplicated and distributed at the school and at the funeral home.

The principal and counselor visited Megan's family again on Monday. Although they were consumed with grief, Megan's parents were also encouraged by the condolences and support they had received from all over the country. There was a groundswell of support for legislation the family had initiated almost immediately after the event, which required that citizens be notified by police when a sexual offender released from the criminal justice system established residence in a given community. The sentiment behind the law reflected the family's understandable determination that "this would not happen to another child." It became a critical and enduring task for the school to support Megan's parents' need for activism without compromising the needs of the other children in the school community—mainly, a return to normalcy. School personnel also needed to avoid becoming involved in the politics of the legislation.

On Tuesday morning, school officials held a meeting with the Department of Education's consultant, a specialist in assisting communities in managing sudden, violent loss. She reinforced the planning that had already taken place. She advised against holding an open community meeting as a forum for the expression of community grief and outrage, citing her experience in several other communities that had experienced losses of a similar magnitude. She described her experience, explaining that despite the best interests of the community officials to maintain order, attendance by several hundred community residents made control of the meetings almost impossible. By the end of the meeting, various institutions in the community had been blamed or scapegoated for the tragedy. In addition, she pointed out, large community meetings attract intense media scrutiny, which tends to increase the emotionality that surrounds them.

A variety of other strategies were outlined to meet the immediate needs of community residents for information and support, although the focus of the school's concerns remained on students and their families. The consultant also encouraged the school to consider carefully the role the media can play in exacerbating or containing a crisis, and she explained the school's legal right to establish limits on access to school property. The administrators decided not to allow media inside the school, but they permitted families to be interviewed on the sidewalk outside the school building, if they chose to. The consultant did support the suggestion that the local cable television channel be used to inform community residents of counseling resources that would continue to be available throughout the summer.

THE FUNERAL

On the evening of the viewing, the school counselor arrived early at the funeral home, where she was joined by a bereavement counselor from the funeral home's staff. A special room had been set aside where they could provide counseling, support and information to those who attended the viewing. This was especially important for the large number of children who had never been to a wake before. Police had roped off the street in front of the funeral home in anticipation of the crowds and this provided an effective degree of control and sense of order at a time when emotions ran high.

The funeral was held that Thursday. To accommodate the outpouring of people who wanted to attend, the Mass was broadcast over a public address system to the overflow crowd that waited outside the church. The presence of uniformed police officers contributed to the somber aura of control that the crowd maintained, despite the intensity of the event. More than 350 people attended the reception held after the funeral, including all the teachers from Megan's school. Again and again the following questions echoed throughout the firehall: "What do we tell our children now?" "How will they feel safe again?" "How will WE feel safe again?" Crisis counselors continued to be available at the school as a resource for worried parents; administrators knew the period of crisis was not over. A week after the funeral, the school counselor canvassed Megan's neighborhood to offer support and assistance, especially reaching out to families whose children had been Megan's playmates.

THE START OF SCHOOL

A week before school started the K. family was again contacted to discuss the needs of their two other school-aged children. The guidance counselor had kept in touch with the family throughout the summer and had provided them with referrals to both family counseling and support groups. Now administrators felt it was important for the family to understand the district's policy of focusing on the needs of the general student population after a tragic loss in the school community. A return to normalcy after a summer of fear was important for the children, many of whom had been restricted from their usual outdoor play activities

by worried and protective parents. Knowing they could count on the predictable, regular school structure and routine would he critical in helping the children put the trauma behind them. The fact that the flag would not be flown at half-mast and there would be no specific memorialization activities were not a reflection of the school's disregard of Megan's death; they were an attempt to return the school community back to "business as usual" as quickly as possible. Megan's parents seemed to understand.

Several days before the scheduled opening of school a special meeting was held for all district staff. The Director of Guidance and Counseling reviewed the activities that had taken place during the summer in response to Megan's death, and a mental health consultant described the ways in which children react to a trauma such as homicide, to help prepare staff. Faculty members were also provided with the opportunity to discuss their reactions to the death. An additional meeting was held for the faculty and staff from Megan's school. Facilitated by a mental health professional from a local mental health center and the State Department of Education's consultant on children and traumatic death, it gave the school personnel who were most acquainted with Megan and extremely affected by her death a chance to share their grief

The guidance counselor from Megan's school was asked to delay her return to classroom activities until October so she could be available to meet with any children who seemed to need assistance because of the trauma. Recognizing that parents might continue to have concerns, a meeting was scheduled for them in mid-October. A mental health professional and members of the local police force answered questions and led a discussion about keeping children safe. The meeting was not well-attended, which school administrators interpreted as a good sign that healing had begun. In November, the local hospice began presenting a puppet show on grief to each grade level ("Good Grief; It's Sky Blue Pink"); the entire school had received the program by fall.

TWO YEARS LATER

Hamilton Township has lost much of the notoriety that engulfed it in the months that followed the death of Megan K., but the community remains indelibly touched by that tragedy. The foundation, started by Megan's family, has donated five scholarships to area high schools since 1994 in Megan's name. Civic groups raised money to demolish the house where she was killed and the property has been converted into a park. And, most notably, the legislation for which her family advocated became law, and is referred to as "Megan's Law." The legislation continues to receive national attention, even, as it becomes the subject of judicial review, and is now a federal law. When it is referenced in the media, a condensed version of Megan's death is often included. It seems clear that this trauma will always remain a defining point in this community's history.

The proactive response strategy enabled the school to organize the resources that were available to community residents in the immediate aftermath of the tragedy, as well as address the more long-term challenges of recovery. This is an example of how clearly defined procedures can be implemented even under extremely traumatic circumstances, and even when school is not in session. It points to the wisdom of designing a crisis response model that identifies and incorporates all the resources the community has to offer.

Maureen M. Underwood, ACSW, LCSW, is the coordinator of a group practice in Morristown, New Jersey. She has written extensively in this area.

Linda Powner, M. Ed., is a consultant to the New Jersey Traumatic Loss in Youth Project and is a retired guidance counselor.

CHILDREN AND POST TRAUMATIC STRESS DISORDER: WHAT CLASSROOM TEACHERS SHOULD KNOW

20

Susan J. Grosse

Post traumatic stress disorder: development of characteristic symptoms following exposure to an extreme traumatic stressor involving direct personal experience of an event that involves actual or threatened death or serious injury, or other threat to ones physical integrity; or witnessing an event that involves death, injury, or a threat to the physical integrity of another person; or learning about unexpected or violent death, serious harm, or threat of death or injury experienced by a family member or other close associate (APA, 1996).

School children may be exposed to trauma in their personal lives or, increasingly, at school. Classroom teachers can help prepare children to cope with trauma by understanding the nature of trauma, teaching children skills for responding to an emergency, and learning how to mitigate the after-effects of trauma.

PTSD RELATED TRAUMA

By the very unexpected nature of trauma, one can never totally prepare for it. And because each individual responds differently to emotional upset, it is impossible to predict trauma after-effects. Under certain circumstances, trauma can induce Post Traumatic Stress Disorder (PTSD). Unrecognized or untreated PTSD can have a lifelong negative impact on the affected individual. Teachers, who spend up to eight hours each day with the children in their charge, can influence the outcome of a child's response to trauma stress by creating an environment in which PTSD is less likely to develop to the point of life impact.

Not all emotionally upsetting experiences will cause PTSD. Trauma sufficient to induce PTSD has specific characteristics and circumstances, including situations
- perceived as life-threatening,
- outside the scope of a child's life experiences,
- not daily, ordinary, normal events,

- during which the child experiences a complete loss of control of the outcome, and
- when death is observed.

Disasters, violence, and accidents are just some of the experiences that can lead to PTSD. Preparing children for trauma involves giving them skills and knowledge to survive the experience and emerge with as little potential as possible for developing PTSD.

SKILLS TO SURVIVE TRAUMATIC EXPERIENCES

Survival skills for traumatic experiences are essentially emergency action plans. Carrying out emergency action plans not only helps a child retain some personal control, but increases the potential for a healthy outcome. Children must know how to:
- Follow directions in any emergency (i.e., stay in their classroom during a lock down)
- Get help in any type of emergency (i.e., dial 911 or call a neighbor)
- Mitigate specific emergencies (i.e., take shelter during a tornado)
- Report the circumstances (i.e., tell an adult if a stranger approaches them or touches them)
- Say "no" and mean it (i.e., firmly shouting "no, don't touch me")

Implementing survival skills requires knowing right and wrong. Children must know or be able to recognize:
- Appropriate vs. inappropriate touching (i.e., shoulder vs. genitals)
- Appropriate vs. inappropriate information sharing (i.e., who is at home at what times)
- Presence of appropriate vs. inappropriate people (i.e., the teacher on playground duty vs. a prowling stranger)

SKILLS TO MITIGATE PTSD

While there is no predictability in who will develop PTSD, it is possible to take steps to prepare children ahead of time and by doing so, lessen the PTSD potential. Children need to be taught lessons about trauma. Learning about people who have experienced trauma and gone on to live healthy lives gives children role models and hope for their own future.

During a traumatic experience, children will survive better if they have a structure to follow and can maintain some sense of control. Learning the survival skills will aid in maintaining this control. Children need accurate and specific information about their immediate safety, about what has happened and about what will happen to them next (James, 1989). Knowledge helps them control their thoughts and feelings.

Following a trauma, debriefing is critical. Children will vary concerning their willingness and readiness to talk about their experiences. Some will play out the event, while others may be more comfortable writing or drawing about the event. What is important is the opportunity to communicate. There are different avenues for the child to communicate, including online discussion forums for children (Sleek, 1998).

A child's initial debriefing should be child-centered and nonjudgmental. The adult should recognize that each child did his or her best, no matter what the outcome, and refrain from offering advice. Adults should recognize that no two children will have the same thoughts, feelings, or opinions. All expressions about the trauma are acceptable.

Following a trauma, it is also important to help a child reestablish control. Reviewing survival skills and drills and planning for "next time" reestablishes strength. Allowing a child to make choices reestablishes their governance over their own lives.

IDENTIFYING PTSD

Everyone reacts to trauma. What differentiates normal reaction from PTSD is the timing of the reaction, its intensity, and the duration of the reaction. Trauma includes emotional as well as physical experiences and injury. Even second-hand exposure to violence can be traumatic. For this reason, all children and adolescents exposed to violence or disaster, even if only through graphic media reports, should be watched for signs of emotional distress (National Institute of Mental Health, 2000).

Symptoms lasting more than one month post trauma may indicate a problem. Specific symptoms to look for include:

- Re-experiencing the event (flashbacks),
- Avoidance of reminders of the event,
- Increased sleep disturbances, and
- Continual thought pattern interruptions focusing on the event.

In children, symptoms may vary with age. Separation anxiety, clinging behavior, or reluctance to return to school may be evident, as may behavior disturbances or problems with concentration. Children may have self doubts, evidenced by comments about body confusion, self-worth, and a desire for withdrawal. As there is no clear demarcation between adolescence and adulthood, adult PTSD symptoms may also evidence themselves in adolescents. These may include recurrent distressing thoughts, sleep disturbances, flashbacks, restricted range of affect, detachment, psychogenic amnesia, increased arousal and hypersensitivity, and increased irritability and outbursts or rage.

HELPING THE CHILD

Making the diagnosis of PTSD requires evaluation by a trained mental health professional. However, regular classroom teachers have a major role in the identification and referral process. Children often express themselves through play. Because the teacher sees the child for many hours of the day including play time, the teacher may be the first to suspect all is not well. Where the traumatic event is known, caregivers can watch for PTSD symptoms. However, traumatic events can involve secrets. Sexual abuse, for example, may take place privately. Sensitive teachers should monitor all children for changes in behavior that may signal a traumatic experience or a flashback to a prior traumatic experience.

Teachers can help a child suspected of post traumatic stress disorder by:
- Gently discouraging reliance on avoidance; letting the child know it is all right to discuss the incident;
- Talking understandingly with the child about their feelings;
- Understanding that children react differently according to age - young children tend to cling, adolescents withdraw;
- Encouraging a return to normal activities;
- Helping restore the child's sense of control of his or her life; and
- Seeking professional help.

Professional assistance is most important since PTSD can have a lifelong impact on a child. Symptoms can lie dormant for decades and resurface many years later during exposure to a similar circumstance. It is only by recognition and treatment of PTSD that trauma victims can hope to move past the impact of the trauma and lead healthy lives. Thus, referral to trained mental health professionals is critical. The school psychologist is a vital resource, and guidance counselors can be an important link in the mental health resource chain.

Although professional assistance is ultimately essential in cases of PTSD, classroom teachers must deal with the immediate daily impact. Becoming an informed teacher is the first step in helping traumatized children avoid the life long consequences of PTSD.

American Psychiatric Association. (1996). *Diagnostic and statistical manual of mental disorders IV.* Washington, DC: American Psychiatric Association.

James, B. (1989). *Treating traumatized children: new insights and creative interventions.* Lexington, MA: D.C. Heath.

National Institute of Mental Health (2000). *Helping children and adolescents cope with violence and disasters.* Washington, DC: NIMH. Available online at http://www.nimh.nih.gov/publicat/violence.cfm

Sleek, S. (1998). After the storm, children play out fears. *APA Monitor,* 29(6). Available online at http://www.apa.org/monitor/jun98/child.html.

Resources Available from ERIC
These resources have been abstracted and are in the ERIC database. Journal articles (EJ) should be available at most research libraries; most documents (ED) are available in microfiche collections at more than 900 locations. Documents can also be ordered though the ERIC Document Reproduction Service (800-443-ERIC).

Demaree, M.A. (1995). Creating safe environments for children with post-traumatic stress disorder. *Dimensions of Early Childhood,* 23(3), 31-33, 40. EJ 501997.

Demaree, M.A. (1994). *Responding to violence in their lives: Creating nurturing environments for children with post-traumatic stress disorder* (conference paper). ED378708.

Dennis, B.L. (1994). *Chronic violence: A silent actor in the classroom.* ED376386.

Karcher, D. R. (1994). *Post-traumatic stress disorder in children as a result of violence: A review of current literature* (doctoral research paper). ED379822.

Motta, R.W. (1994). Identification of characteristics and causes of childhood posttraumatic stress disorder. *Psychology in the Schools,* 31(1), 49-56. EJ480780.

Richards, T., & Bates, C. (1997). Recognizing post-traumatic stress in children. *Journal of School Health,* 67(10), 441-443. EJ561961.

Other Resources
American Academy of Child and Adolescent Psychiatry, 3615 Wisconsin Avenue, NW, Washington, DC, 20016-3007, 202-966-7300, http://www.aacap.org

American Psychiatric Association, 1400 K Street, NW, Washington, DC 20005, 202-682-6000; http://www.psych.org

American Psychological Association, 750 First Street, NE, Washington, DC 20002, 202-336-5500, http://www.apa.org

Anxiety Disorders Association of America (ADAA), 11900 Parklawn Drive, Suite 100, Rockville, MD 20852, 301-231-9350; http://www.adaa.org

Disaster Stuff for Kids, http://www.jmu.edu/psychologydept/4kids.htm

Federal Emergency Management Agency http://www.fema.gov/kids

International Society for Traumatic Stress Studies (ISTSS), 60 Revere Drive, Suite 500, Northbrook, IL 60062, http://www.istss.org

National Center for Kids Overcoming Crisis, (includes *Healing Magazine* online) 1-800-8KID-123, http://www.kidspeace.org/facts

National Center for PTSD, 215 N. Main Street, White River Junction, VT 05009; 802-296-5132; http://www.ncptsd.org/

National Center for Post-Traumatic Stress Disorder of the Department of Veterans Affairs http://www.ncptsd.org/

National Institute for Mental Health (NIMH) 6001 Executive Boulevard, Rm 8184, MSC 9663, Bethesda, MD 20892-9663; 301-4513, Hotline 1-88-88-ANXIETY, http://www.nimh.nih.gov

ERIC Digests are funded by the Office (OERI) of the US Department of Education. Digests are fully reproducible. Find this digest and others on the web at http://www.eric.ed.gov

Reprinted with permission from "Helping People Cope with Tragedy & Grief," published by ERIC Counseling and Student Services Clearinghouse.

Susan J. Grosse, ERIC Clearinghouse on Teaching and Teacher Education, ERIC Clearinghouse on Counseling and Student Services, and ERIC Digest.

DEALING WITH ACCIDENTAL STUDENT DEATH

21

Barbara L. Korpos

Most of us are faced with the question of what to do when tragedy strikes at least once during our careers. We need to remember that there is only one wrong thing to do, and that is to do nothing. We all shared in the common tragedy of September 11th on many different levels and to varying degrees. We all dealt with the event as best we could given our different circumstances.

We also share the potential for traumatic accidental death of a student, as happened at Roxbury High School in January of 2001. Because we never know just when such an event might take place, it is important to develop a plan of action beforehand. This critical resource enables one to act quickly and decisively if and when tragedy strikes. The following is a brief overview of the procedures undertaken at Roxbury last year as a tragedy occurred outside of school.

- Principal notifies other administrators to review situation once report is verified
- Secretary alerts bus company and secures additional teacher substitutes
- Director of Student Personnel Services contacts school counselors, school social worker and psychologist, SAC and nurse (Crisis Team)
- Faculty phone chain is initiated sharing brief summary of situation and facts to date
- Other schools previously attended by victim and siblings notified
- Victim's schedule reviewed, cumulative folder and locker secured
- Crisis Team meets to hear specific information, determine responsibilities and locations for large/small group crisis counseling
- Department supervisors, lead teachers and class advisors meet with Crisis Team
- Outside agency crisis counselors secured along with local clergy
- Principal meets with faculty and support personnel to advise procedures and distribute incident statement to be read in homerooms
- Counselors and CST members compile "at risk" student list, contact parents
- Victim's counselor available to sit in his/her classes throughout day
- Absentees contacted to determine reason for absence
- Sign-in/out sheets provided in all counseling areas
- Water, juice and light snacks available in counseling areas
- Support services and refreshments made available for faculty in separate location
- Consistent monitoring of students and faculty throughout day and days immediately following event
- Announcement of situation and list of school support activities prepared to be mailed home
- Debriefing of faculty at end of day to express concerns, update "at risk" list and announce funeral arrangements

With each successive day, the need for counseling services should begin to diminish to the point of students being accommodated by their individual counselors. Students should be encouraged to express and label their feelings while counselors should be mindful of both verbal and nonverbal communication. Specific attention should be given to student concerns about peers and invitations extended to them to join the next session. Counselors are reminded to listen to feelings more than content, and refrain from minimizing or discounting the student's tale. Above all, be genuine and honest, know your limits, and refer to your resources when necessary.

A discussion regarding funeral etiquette and expectations is extremely helpful, as many students have never experienced a funeral before. Parents should be encouraged to attend the services with their children or accompanying a small group of friends. Faculty members will be in attendance as well, but should not be expected to supervise students. Other continuing discussions should include returning to normalcy and daily routine for the purpose of getting on with the business of life. This is not to say that we should no longer remember or reflect, but that stability needs to be reinstated.

Follow-up services at Roxbury included evening sessions for parents and students together as well as separately. These services occurred shortly after the incident and several weeks later. Procedures regarding memorializing the victim should be established by the administration and relayed gently but firmly to the students. As anniversaries occur, students need to be discouraged from breaking normal routines. Parental contacts are helpful in this endeavor.

An excellent resource book of forms, checklists and other suggestions is *Managing Sudden Traumatic Loss In The Schools* by Maureen M. Underwood and Karen Dunne-Maxim.

Barbara L. Korpos, M.A., is a school counselor at Roxbury High School, Succasunna, NJ.

CRISIS RESPONSE PLANS REVIEWED AFTER SCHOOL SHOOTINGS

Counseling Today, Shawn M. Schmitt

It's a typical day in a high school classroom. Students are going about their usual agendas—working on geometry homework, reading plays in English class, dabbling in chemistry.

Suddenly, it happens. Shots ring out. Quick. Loud. Resonant.

The students are suddenly aware their school is under siege.

Would they know what to do or how to get out? And after it's over, would they know where they could seek counseling? But most importantly, could it have been avoided?

Following the tragic shootings of 12 high school students and a teacher at Columbine High School in Littleton, Colo., many school officials are asking themselves the same questions, but many only have a shadow of a crisis response plan in their district manuals, while others simply haven't explored the notion of creating a plan to save lives, said Judy Davidson, director of Renew Center for Personal Recovery in Berea, Ky.

"A lot of schools are doing various pieces of it. I feel there are many schools ahead of others, but there are very few that have all of these pieces in place comfortably," she said. "This is an ongoing process. Many (school) systems are just now learning how to do different pieces."

According to Davidson, many school districts are using outdated crisis response plans that simply deal with the aftermath of a tragic event rather than building measures into their plans that call for proactive steps to deal with the mental well-being of students.

"Prevention ... includes a system of identifying those at risk, and it has to be done by staff who have their blinders off," she said. "We have not taken indicators seriously in many cases because many times we have preconceived notions of who is at risk. It's clear we've overlooked emotional intelligence in our schools and the impact of bullying and sexual harassment. That's crisis intervention, that's crisis prevention."

But even the best laid plans couldn't have stopped the tragedy that unfolded at Columbine, said Carol Hacker, a former Columbine school counselor who helped draft the high school's crisis response plan.

"The [school] district has a good crisis plan, but that's not the problem. This couldn't have been avoided, even with the best crisis plan in the world," she said, noting more than 150 school district staff, faculty, and administration were trained yearly on what to do if an emergency should arise. "We never had anything of this magnitude."

Regardless, all schools should have a plan, Hacker said, and all plans should encompass all sorts of possible crises. "You need to get to know your community resources and prescreen community people," she said. "[Schools] can't do it alone, that's why they have to prescreen and know who will help."

A TEAM EFFORT

School administrators and employees are many times the first to notice if a student is troubled, and it's important for any response plan to include a description of children who may be at-risk or capable of violent behavior, according to the U.S. Center for Mental Health Services (CMHS). The plan also should include step-by-step procedures to aid students who seem violent or feel alienated.

However, CMHS officials said, any plan should have the full support of the local school board and families in the community. Plus, the plan should be compliant with federal, state, and local laws.

"There are many, many lessons that can be learned from these school shootings," Davidson said. "Low-level trauma that is cumulative, like bullying or being shunned—that leads children to feelings of not belonging—can lead to these major events."

One of the ways the response plans can be created and initiated is by way of a response team that can oversee the preventive measures, and in some cases, coor-

91

dinate a proper response following a tragedy, said Patricia Henderson, director of guidance for Northside Independent School District in San Antonio, Texas.

Oftentimes, a group that already works with the school administration or school board can add these duties to their workload; or, a new group can be formed. Nevertheless, everyone in the community should feel comfortable with the plan so they can have peace of mind knowing their school children are safe.

"I recommend a counselor and administrator sit down and develop a plan," Henderson said. "A team of leadership from the campus, including the counselors, need to meet and decide how to proceed. And, [the team] needs to keep the staff informed of facts of the matter."

According to CMHS, a wide-array of leaders from all facets of the community should be involved with the implementation of a team and a response plan, including parent group leaders; law enforcement personnel; clergy; physicians and nurses; the media; attorneys, judges and probation officers; mental health and child welfare personnel; violence prevention group representatives; business leaders; family agency and family resource center staff; youth workers and volunteers; local elected and non-elected officials; recreation, cultural, and arts organizations staff; college or university faculty; members of local advisory boards; interest group representatives; and other members of the community who may be influential.

"There needs to be a plan, and the school and community should work together on that program," said Joanne McDaniel, research director for Center for the Prevention of School Violence in Raleigh, N.C. "We've done a good job getting information out in the past year about warning signs; now we need to work on a timely response."

In addition, it's important to delegate responsibilities early on so everyone knows what prospective roles to play should a tragedy occur, said Janice Gallagher, president-elect of the American School Counselor Association (ASCA).

"People should have specific responsibilities, such as, who is going to be the media spokesperson," said Gallagher. "The plan should be put together ahead of time by parties who are stakeholders in the community."

A UNIQUE PLAN

Just like the air-raid drills from decades ago, some school districts are beginning to implement unique drills to train students how to respond if violence erupts in their schools. From taking protective cover to

learning where the nearest exits are, these plans are sure to save lives, McDaniel said.

Plus, she said, code words that indicate that there is serious trouble within the school could be announced on the school's communication systems to give teachers and students an early warning without causing wide-spread panic. Local law enforcement also should be notified immediately.

"We need to practice our crisis management, just like they practice fire drills," McDaniel said. "Kids should know what to do, whether to hit the floor or head for the exits. This practice is not meant to scare people, but to help ... schools need to present it in a right way — not in a way to alarm, but in a way to reassure."

In fact, it may be best if the drills did not include a certain scenario, such as a school shooting, Gallagher said. "Just continue evacuating the buildings like there's a fire drill. I wouldn't set up any scenarios. I've heard of people doing things like that, but I wouldn't do any mock-up tragedy."

Also, the plans should be tailor-fit to suit different school districts. Different schools—depending on topography, region, or the wealth of the district—should have slightly different plans.

Following the Littleton shootings, Henderson said some students reacted differently within her school district. Northside Independent School District is somewhat unique in that it encompasses different neighborhoods, from wealthy to poor; from peaceful to violent; from urban to rural, she said.

"We noticed in the aftermath of [Littleton] that schools in our district that have experienced more violence reacted less dramatically than the upper-middle class neighborhood schools," she said, noting the response plans will be basically the same in most districts with a few minor changes to adapt different circumstances.

McDaniel said she believes in instituting the "four S's," which could be worked into response plans:

* Statistics — Learning both the school's and the students' strengths and weaknesses

* Sight Assessments — Understanding the physical environment of the school

* Surveys — These can show how the students and staff feel about the safety of their school

* Students — Knowing and understanding the students is important, as well as giving them opportunities to connect with counselors, staff, and administration

"Every school has a unique set of characteristics and resources to draw upon. They need to know where their strengths are and where they have problem areas," McDaniel said. "Every school has to have a good understanding of itself and its population."

Davidson also agreed surveys and safety audits should be in place for a response plan to work effectively. Plus, she said, the plan should be "building specific" and address all potential incidents, including natural disasters, medical emergencies, and events that could put students and staff at risk of violence or death.

"We have to deal with all of those areas. I think Littleton is an example of what could be happening all over the country," Davidson said, adding schools also should have a more secure system in place to screen visitors. "Many schools have plans that are outdated and narrow in focus."

All school personnel, including bus drivers, cafeteria workers and janitors should be made aware of the plans as well. "These people play a key role. The janitor is probably the only person who knows where the gas and water cut-offs are," Gallagher said.

According to Gallagher, all schools in Texas— where she served as director of student advocacy services in San Antonio— are mandated to have a crisis response plan. However, she said, even the best plan probably couldn't have prevented the Littleton shootings.

"I don't think anything is perfect. But you have to review the plans periodically, whether you have a disaster or not," she said. "You have to have training. You can't say, 'Here's the plan,' and stick it on a principal's wall."

However, not only does Hacker suggest using code words to indicate trouble, but she supports the use of color-coded paper to alert teachers to imminent danger to keep students from panicking.

"If teachers get a message on a certain colored paper, they know there's an emergency," she said.

While she did concede the color-coding wouldn't work during a crisis that leaves no response time for school officials, she said it would help during natural disasters, such as tornadoes. Currently there are three school districts using the color-coding, Hacker said.

THE AFTERMATH

Should a tragedy occur, counselors need to be on-hand to tackle post-traumatic or residual effects. Children and staff are significantly traumatized by quick, violent episodes and will need intensive, long-time support and assistance, experts say.

"It's important for counselors to fall back on skills they may not use on a daily basis," McDaniel said.

Currently, many school counselors are overburdened by administrative chores and aren't able to focus on proactive measures such as counseling and mediation. According to statistics provided by the U.S. Department of Education, there is one counselor to handle the problems of 513 students across the nation.

ACA endorses a 250-to-1 ratio, which would give students more access to mental health services.

"What we have to have in place is recognition that time moves forward and these emotions move forward. We need to recognize that out of crises can come learning experiences," McDaniel said. "(Counselors) need to be given opportunities by the (school) administration to perform the counseling they were trained to do."

CMHS officials say several steps should be taken during the aftermath of a tragedy, including helping parents understand children's reactions to violence; helping teachers and other staff deal with their reactions to the crisis; helping students and faculty adjust after the crisis; and helping victims and family members of victims re-enter the school environment.

"Eventually the school needs to be back in a situation where they stand on their own," McDaniel said. "We have to be ready to address these crises, however great they are in magnitude."

Counselors also have to be concerned about the suicide rate following tragedies, Davidson said. "We need to worry about post-traumatic isolation," she said. "We're so focused on the plan that we may fail to respond appropriately in these other areas."

And, after a full day of providing counseling services following a violent tragedy, counselors should be prepared to perform a debriefing with staff and administration, according to Gallagher.

"You need to debrief at the end of the day and formulate plans for the next day. Ask 'What was right? What was wrong? What do we need to work on?'" she said. "I don't think we could've planned for Littleton, but I do think all the signs were there."

Shawn M. Schmitt is a staff writer for ACA's monthly newspaper, Counseling Today. This article originally appeared in the June, 1999 issue.

Counseling Today, Peter Guerra

The deadly shootings at Columbine High School in Littleton, Colo., on April 20 has prompted schools, parents, students, and counselors to call for preventative measures to stop similar tragedies in the future. ACA joined those in expressing their grief and called for improvements in dealing with at-risk youth (See sidebar "How ACA responds to a crisis" on this page).

"The American Counseling Association expresses its extreme sadness regarding the terrible tragedy in Littleton, Colorado," said ACA President Loretta Bradley. "We are horrified by the unthinkable violence occurring in our nation's schools, and we seek to help bring an end to these deadly outbursts."

Bradley called for preventative measures to be instituted so that tragedies like this one could be avoided in the future.

"We can't simply try to pick up the pieces after a school and community have been devastated by one of these shootings," she said. "We need to provide guidance and support to our children and youth early. We should be providing them with the preventive services they need on an ongoing, everyday basis, to prevent outbreaks of violence from occurring in the first place."

Bradley sent a letter to the 90 ACA members in the Littleton, Colo., area, which is printed on this page, and also sent a letter to the Jefferson County Board of Education. In the letter, Bradley expressed her sympathy for the tragedy on behalf of ACA members around the world.

COLUMBINE COUNSELORS RESPOND

According to Carol Hacker, a former school counselor at Columbine High School and an ACA member, the school counselors had a reasonable crisis response plan in place. Hacker was called up on the day of the shooting to help counsel children and parents at the elementary school where they gathered on April 20. She described the scene at the elementary school as "chaotic" because of the confusion surrounding what was hap-

pening. She said that after the students from Columbine were led off of the bus to the elementary school, they were interviewed by police and then provided with medical treatment or crisis counseling. The students were then put on the elementary schools' stage so that parents could identify their kids and take them home.

"It was heartbreaking, because as the day went on, there were parents who seemed to know that their kid wasn't going to appear on stage," she said. In such cases, Hacker assigned a victims counselor to the family to provide any assistance the family needed.

Hacker said that the crisis response plan the school had was a good one, but on this occasion, not enough.

"We had a good crisis response plan in place, but we didn't expect anything like this," she said.

Hacker had praise for the teachers, custodians, lunch workers, and other school employees who helped kids get out of the cafeteria during the shootings. Diaries of the gunmen found days after the shooting indicated that they planned on the time of day for their attack so that the lunch room would be completely full and they would be able to kill as many students as possible. Yet Hacker said that the lunch room was almost empty by the time the gunmen made their way to the cafeteria.

She said that after the shooting started, lunch workers and custodians grabbed children and herded them out of school or locked them in closets and lockers. She estimated that the shootings would have been a lot worse had it not been for these school employees risking their lives to get children out of the cafeteria.

Hacker also said that teachers locked kids in closets, made students hide under desks, and tried to get as many students out of the school to safety. One teacher, William Sanders, was fatally shot while directing students down a smoke-filled hallway to safety. Some students reported that Sanders had an opportunity to escape but stayed to help other students get out of the building.

There was also high praise for the Columbine High School students in the wake of the shootings. Hacker described a meeting at a local church that the Columbine students called themselves on April 22 to discuss the shootings. She reported that around 2,500 students and parents showed up at the church that evening, and discussed their feelings surrounding the shootings. Hacker said that the students requested that media not come to the meeting and said it was respected. Of the meeting, Hacker said it was very therapeutic for the students.

"It was a wonderful, healing thing to do" she said of the meeting. "Kids came together at the church and just talked to each other."

And Hacker praised the efforts of the Columbine school counselors, school psychologists, and social workers who worked diligently to help the students and parents deal with the initial shock of this event.

"The school counselors have been incredible here, as well as the school social workers and psychologists," she said. "They came in on their day off and worked hours and hours and have gone way beyond what you would expect."

Hacker said the children and parents of Columbine are dealing with a mountain of issues right now, including posttraumatic stress disorder, anger, and fear.

"There are kids with abandoned survivor guilt, who held Mr. Sanders in their arms for three hours and then were forced to leave," she said. "Also, some kids feel guilty that they survived while some of their friends did not."

Asked how the community was coping in the wake of this tragedy, Hacker said "We are doing well, but long-term I don't know what will happen."

Victims counselors from the Red Cross were on hand immediately following the shooting to help victims and their families to cope with the sudden trauma. However Dan Mosley, chair of the Disaster Mental Health Service Team of the Mile High Red Cross, said that it was important to approach trauma victims with caution and not to be too intrusive.

"Victims of trauma or loss don't necessarily need five counselors breathing down their necks," he told CNN. If he saw a student crying, Mosley said he would approach the student and say something like, "I'm with the Red Cross, and we're here to see how we can help. I wouldn't say, 'I'm a shrink.'"

The mental health efforts for the community are being coordinated by the Jefferson County Mental Health center, with help from the Mental Health Association of Colorado. The Mile High Red Cross has also started the "Community Healing Fund," which as of April 21 had already raised close to $100,000 for victim assistance.

CALLS FOR CHANGE

In response to the deadly shootings at Littleton, Colo., on April 20, schools, parents, and politicians have called for increasing counselors and conflict resolution programs, decreasing children's access to guns and violent content on television, and refocusing the nation on the problems of today's youth.

President Clinton, speaking at T.C. Williams High School in Alexandria, Va. on April 22, said that he would like to see more counselors, as proposed by the U.S. Conference of Mayors during last October's conference on school safety (See "President joins city mayors in calling for more school counselors," November 1998, *Counseling Today*).

"There is really nothing more important than keeping our schools safe," Clinton said. "And we've tried to do a lot of things in that regard over the last few year—having a zero tolerance for guns and drugs policy, putting new community police officers in schools where they're needed, trying to support more counselors in schools, more after-school, more mentoring programs, more conflict resolution programs."

The president spoke with the Alexandria high school students involved in a unique conflict resolution program. The program involves peer mediators, school counselors, teachers, and school administrators. The peer mediators respond to students who need help and report to the school counselors and to the administrators any serious conflicts that arise in the school. The program allows kids to resolve some of their own crises, a move that many believe will help students come forward to talk about their problems instead of letting problems fester within them.

The president also allocated $1.5 million in federal aid to Littleton to help victims pay for funerals, medical expenses, lost wages, and counseling.

Attorney General Janet Reno also commented on the need for counselors, and has sent a crisis response team to Littleton, Colo., that included victims counselors.

"We've got to get guns out of the hands of young people," Reno said at a press conference on April 21. "We've got to make sure they have the counseling, the support to help them come to grips with the anger of their life when it occurs."

There are many people who are pointing fingers at causes for the shootings, including violence in the media, accessibility of guns by children, and lack of parental outreach to their kids.

However, Hillary Rodham Clinton pointed the finger squarely at America's "culture of violence" in a speech on April 22. Speaking to the New York State United Teachers, the first lady was particularly tough on video games, describing them as military training for impressionable minds.

"We have to be willing to talk about the culture of violence that infects the lives of our children," she said, according to the article "First Lady Denounces 'Culture of Violence'" in the April 23 *Washington Post*. "The constant exposure to violence on TV, in the movies, on video games, in music—there's much too much evidence that children get desensitized."

To help educators and parents identify any warning signs for students at-risk for violence, the Department of Education published "Early Warning, Timely Response: A Guide to Safe Schools" last year in an effort to prevent the type of school shootings that occurred last school year. The guide gives parents and educators tips on identifying and helping students at-risk of violence. The guide is available from ACA's website at www.counseling.org/schoolviolence.

With the recent rash of school shootings occurring across this nation, schools and parents are going to have to come up with ways to identify and help schools to prevent this type of violence from happening again. In an upcoming issue of *Counseling Today*, there will be articles on crisis plans, debates on the role of the school counselor, and practice tips for counselors in identifying and treating at-risk youth.

For now, the people of Littleton, Colo., will have to cope with tragedy of April's events. Carol Hacker said on April 26 that the counselors in the surrounding schools are trying to deal with student fears and anxieties in the wake of the shootings. She said that school counselors are doing their best to try to allay these fears.

"We have to call in reinforcements because our resources are drawing thin," she said. "Kids are fearing that something similar will happen in their school."

HOW ACA RESPONDS TO A CRISIS

In the hours and days immediately following the tragedy at Columbine High School, ACA responded to media calls, issued statements, and made articles on violence in the schools available. A new website, www.counseling.org/schoolviolence, was created to help provide information on preventing school violence for parents, schools, and students. Also, ACA

President Loretta Bradley sent letters to the Jefferson County Board of Education and to the 90 ACA members that live in the Columbine area. The text of the letter to the ACA members is included on this page.

ACA Manager of Public Communications Cheryl Haas also worked long hours preparing press releases, gathering materials to give to media, and coordinating media interviews. Overall, Haas received more than 100 media calls and 10 ACA members spoke to media outlets on school violence and counseling.

In addition, ACA Interim Executive Director Richard Yep coordinated efforts to provide assistance to the students, parents, and counselors in the Columbine area with Nancy Perry, executive director of the American School Counselors Association (ASCA).

"We were saddened by the tragedy in Littleton and know that many students across the country will be asking lots of questions for many months to come," Yep said. "For the parents, counselors, and teachers who will be faced with these questions or other situations, ACA felt that we had an obligation to provide information and resources as quickly as possible. In addition to the initial wave of calls we received from the media, we placed several pieces of information on our website at www.counseling.org and via our toll free member service phone number at 800.347.6647 ext. 222. While we certainly cannot provide all of the answers, our hope is that as a professional counseling association, we will be able to provide materials, and to act as a facilitator, for those who seek services to help during this terrible time."

Howard Smith, Senior Director of Professional Affairs, wrote up a question and answer document for students, parents, and school counselors on how to respond to questions about the shooting. An excerpt is printed on this page.

"In terms of what is needed, people are going to talk things out, to talk about your feelings, worries, and concerns. And that means that teachers are going to have to help kids with that but it also means that someone is going to have to train the teachers, and the teachers and counselors in the school are also going to need help themselves," he said. "The helpers need help too."

— Bob Dingman, an ACA member and an expert on disaster counseling in Virginia Beach, Va.

"The kids were giving off signals that the adults in their lives should have, and could have, seen. This should be a

wake-up call to everyone that has or works with kids to pay attention. Adults, parents, and teachers need to know that their school counselors are resources to them. If parents or teachers see strange behaviors they should contact their school counselor. That's what they're there for."

— Patricia Henderson, school counselor
in San Antonio, Texas and an ACA member

"The reign of terror that exists in many American schools will never be effectively combated with secondary prevention measures such as weapon searches. What the schools urgently need to do now is to use the primary prevention programs that are available but are seldom used. These pro- *grams target the aggressive antecedents of weapon violence, such as bullying and severe teasing, that begin in the primary grades. When allowed to go unchecked, bullying and severe teasing have driven many children to kill their tormentors, bystanders, and then themselves."*

— Dorothea Ross, counselor in Bainbridge
Island, Wash., and an ACA member

Peter Guerra is a former editor of ACA's monthly newspaper, Counseling Today. *This article originally appeared in the May, 1999 issue.*

Section Four

Counseling Strategies, Coping Tips

What Murder Leaves Behind: Special Considerations In The Treatment Of Surviving Family Members

24

Robert S. Fink

There is a familiar Yiddish expression, "Everyone has tsuris." In short, everyone has his or her sorrows, losses and traumas. At a deeper level, it suggests that everyone's suffering of loss and trauma shares much in common and also that everyone's suffering is steeped in meaning that is very personal and idiosyncratic. As counselors, we are dramatically confronted with this dialectic of common and unique experiences of traumatic loss when we counsel the survivor-victims of murder.

One meaning of murder for surviving family members is the loss of a loved one through death, albeit a sudden and unexpected one. Murder, however, also represents the "ultimate violation" (Bard & Sangrey, 1986). It etches in the minds of survivor-victims a terrifying awareness of the reality of extreme cruelty, amorality, willful malicious action, and destruction of the self without warning. Murder also infuses surviving family members with a disturbing sense of the terror and helplessness of the victim. It is these ultimate violation qualities of murder that underlie the unique aspects of the experience for survivors. Also, it is these ultimate violation experiences that confront counselors with special challenges as they help survivor-victims cope with violent loss.

This chapter explores some of the special needs that survivor-victims bring to counseling and presents therapeutic perspectives and strategies for working with these issues. Special attention is directed to: 1) the interplay of trauma and grief; 2) traumatic memory reenactment; 3) moral ambiguity and complexity; 4) profound change in worldview; 5) question of closure; and 6) countertransference. What follows is not a comprehensive treatment protocol for survivor-victims of murder. It is a selective focus on approaches aimed at helping survivor-victims learn to not be dominated by their experience of murder, but rather to live around and through it.

The Interplay of Trauma and Loss Reactions

Survivor-victims experience an intertwined set of loss and trauma responses to the murder of a family member. Loss reactions pull toward the deceased, searching for a psychological and physical connection. They are experienced as feelings of pining (sadness, grief, depression, separation anxiety), thoughts of connection or reunion, and searching actions. Trauma reactions, to the contrary, are marked by a pulling away from memories of the deceased, in particular from memories of the way the family member died. Features of trauma reactions include intense feelings of fear (panic, terror, dissociation), intrusive thoughts and images of the violent manner of death, and avoidance of traumatizing stimuli (Schillace, 2000). These reactions, although intertwined, are very contradictory and difficult to psychologically consider at once. Rynearson (2001) vividly describes this dilemma: "Separation distress draws toward an embracing reunion with the person's vitality, while trauma distress dreads and avoids the imaginary witnessing of the person's dying…. One response pulls toward, while the other pushes away, the memory of the deceased (p.25)."

The survivor-victim needs to grieve and deal with the traumatic distress. It is important for the counselor to respond to both types of reactions. I have worked with many survivor-victims who have had previous counseling related to the murder of a family member. Often, the previous work has taken the form of grief counseling, without actively addressing the trauma reaction. Although helpful, such an exclusive approach tends to limit a client's movement in dealing with both the loss and trauma reactions.

Part of the counselor's task here is to help survivors understand the intertwined nature of their emotional reactions. Clients frequently worry that their unpredictable cycles of emotional states (intense waves of emotion, feeling nothing, feeling "normal but with shades of gray") mean that they are breaking down. They experience an incoherence in their reactions and tend to have little frame of reference for understanding their responses. One important set of interventions involves explanations that serve to enhance the client's understanding. It is helpful to educate clients on the nature of trauma and loss reactions, and the contradictory pulls that they exert on their functioning and feelings. It helps clients to understand that these reactions are simultaneous responses to the murder of their family member, that they vary in intensity, and the trauma reaction is likely to be the more intense and dominant response for a number of months after the event. It is useful for clients to understand that reactions to loss and trauma are highly individual. There is no sequential set of stages through which people go. Later in counseling, it helps clients to understand that, although loss reactions have become predominant, trauma responses will recur at times.

A second set of interventions is concerned with helping clients to modulate their intense distress. This focus has particular value for clients who are preoccupied with intrusive images of violent death, as well as for those who lack a strong capacity for self-soothing and affect tolerance or have limited social support. Interventions here deal with relaxation and cognitive management. An enhanced capacity for relaxation can be facilitated through training in deep breathing or progressive relaxation exercises, guided imagery or meditation. Clients differ as to what kind of relaxation strategies work for them. In vivo training and ongoing practice are crucial. Cognitive management techniques include exercises in stopping negative or traumatic thoughts and substituting thoughts and coping statements that draw on the client's capacity for resiliency and confidence (Rynearson, 2001). Success in these relaxation and cognitive management techniques can help clients to manage their intense distress and arousal more effectively, as well as teach more flexible forms of avoidance.

A final set of interventions speaks to the clinical issue of countering the intensity of clients' traumatic distress by stimulating associations to the living vitality of the deceased. Rynearson (2001) recommends questions such as: "What would X say that you need right now?; Tell me about X.; Do you have any pictures of X?" Activities such as bringing in photographs or belongings are also helpful. The purpose of these interventions is to connect the client more actively with memories of the deceased's living and well-being, and simultaneously moderate the traumatic preoccupations.

TRAUMATIC MEMORY REENACTMENT

As noted above, survivors commonly experience trauma reactions as part of their response to a family member's murder. This is true even for those who were not directly exposed to the murder and/or would not meet the diagnostic criteria for PTSD. Recent research (Rynearson, 2001) indicates that trauma reactions typically are ongoing and intense for several months after the event. This research also suggests that approximately 30 percent of survivors continue to suffer from intense traumatic distress for years afterwards. This recurrent and unproductive traumatic memory reenactment represents the "reexperiencing" symptoms described in the DSM-IV. Meichenbaum (1994) characterizes this situation as one in which "trauma stops the chronological clock and fixes the traumatic in memory and imagination" (p.378). The challenge for the counselor is to help the client construct a trauma narrative. In other words, to take the fragments of overwhelming experience and to "tell and retell his/her story so the events can be given a place in his/her life history, in his/her autobiography...The traumatic events need to be put into a story, placed in time with a beginning, middle and end." (Meichenbaum, 1994, p.378)

A brief analysis of traumatic memory reenactment will serve to illuminate the constructive trauma narrative to be discussed below. Significant parts of the stress that survivors experience derive from the immediacy and physicality of the murder, and their identification with the terror and helplessness of the victim. They feel like helpless witnesses to the event, or they become immersed in compensatory action fantasies of remorse, retaliation and/or overprotection (Rynearson, 2001). In any event, the sense of being a helpless witness or the compulsion to take actions to reattach to the deceased maintains the immediacy of the traumatic memory reenactment.

Constructive trauma narrative is described in slightly different terms by therapist-writers (Herman, 1997; James, 1988; Meichenbaum, 1994; Rynearson, 2001; Steele, 1997) depending on their theoretical persuasion and the populations with which they work. However, the common core of this approach is that the counselor structures an experience that assists the clients to tell the story of the murder in considerable detail and the story of their experience of it. Frequently, the client will be encouraged to bring in possessions of the deceased or draw pictures, which may stimulate associations to the murder experience and the living memories. The counselor asks trauma-specific questions that give an evocative temporal structure to the experience. These questions are both general (e.g., "Tell me what happened. When did it happen? Start at the beginning of the incident and then move through it to the end" (Meichenbaum, 1994). These latter questions deal with particulars of the experience and often are based on sensory experience, reflecting the reality that overwhelming stress is often processed largely as a sensory experience (Steele, 1997). Examples of these questions (Steele, 1997) include asking clients about their sensory memories of the incident, their fears and worries, their anger and fantasies of revenge, their relationship with the deceased, and things they wish they had done differently.

This work needs to be done in the context of a safe and sensitive counseling relationship. Within this context the counselor takes considerable initiative to acknowledge the murder experience and structure the trauma-specific work. It should be done during the first part of the session, so that time is left to process the experience and deal with emotional distress stimulated by the experience.

The following case example illustrates many of these issues. Mrs. A came for counseling several months after her husband, a union leader, had been stabbed to death in his office by a disgruntled union member. She complained in particular of depression, haunting intrusive images of her husband bleeding to death on a floor and persistent guilt that she should have been there with him. As we constructed the trauma narrative, many details emerged that had not been part of her earlier repetitive and more fragmented story. Two were especially significant. First, her husband had written the murderer's name in blood on the floor. Second, she imagined that her husband was lying on the floor paralyzed with terror, knowing that he was dying. As we threaded this narrative together, it became apparent that her husband's dying actions had been heroic. The counselor then asked her what she wished she had been able to say to him in those last moments, and how he would have replied. Among other things, she wished to apologize for not saving him or being there to comfort him. His response, in part, acknowledged her feelings, asked her to try to live well in the future and expressed his satisfaction that justice would be done.

This experience brought considerable relief to Mrs. A and a notable reduction in the intensity of her traumatic reaction. It permitted her to process many aspects of the experience that had been inaccessible and disturbing. Also, it assisted her in developing a more coherent narrative of the incident and a revised relationship to the dying scene. Finally, it was one step in stimulating a renewed connection with the vitality and kindness that her husband had brought to their life together.

MORAL AMBIGUITY AND COMPLEXITY

Family members of a murder victim are compelled to confront the moral ambiguity and complexity of extreme situations. They may feel that they have been confronted with the face of evil in the person of the murderer. They are apt to have revenge fantasies. These fantasies may be intense, preoccupying and raise disturbing questions for survivors about their desire and capacity to harm others. They may carry out acts of revenge (usually small and indirect) toward others whom they associate with the murderer: family, lawyers, or people of a certain racial/ethnic background. Survivors (and others) may entertain questions about the victim's role in what happened. They may have concerns about their possible complicity; did certain actions or inaction on their part contribute to the victim's vulnerability?

These issues need to be actively attended to with care and sensitivity in counseling. Frequently the client may be reluctant to bring them up directly. Often they may be a basis for significant guilt. If not dealt with, they may be a source of troublesome maladaptive behavior.

The task for the counselor is to take a position of 'bearing witness." In short, the counselor must strive to suspend preconceived judgments and help the clients come to a detailed understanding of what they did, what the victim did, and the reasons for their self blame or anger at others (Herman, 1997). This process may involve helping survivors to accept that they may not have done all that they could have; or that the victim may have taken risks. Understanding this does not absolve the criminal of responsibility, but it may help survivors to find a balance between guilt/ blame and denial as they review their actions and those of the victim.

The case of Z illustrates the critical importance of bearing witness. Z sought counseling 18 months after his father and uncle were murdered at their store. He came with complaints of depression, preoccupation with the murders, and uncharacteristic lashing out in anger at family members. He had sought counseling several months earlier. It had been moderately helpful. During the initial counseling, he had briefly mentioned his concerns about the dangerous location of the store and his avoidance of the topic with his father. Also, Z discussed, in an idealizing manner, how his father had kept a loaded gun locked in the store safe. The first counselor reassured him that neither he nor his father was at fault and that we cannot ultimately protect ourselves from a determined sociopath. During the second session, the counselor pressed Z to expand on his concerns. Quite emotionally, he examined his guilt that he had been frightened to confront his father. Also, Z explored, with strong emotion, his disappointment and sense of betrayal that his father, who had always stressed being cautious and wary of others, had taken an ambivalent stance in response to the danger of the neighborhood. This work helped significantly diminish Z's traumatic reaction and anger, and facilitated his taking a more compassionate view of his father, himself and their conflicts about dealing honestly with danger.

Taking this position of "bearing witness" can be challenging for counselors, given our sensitivity to blaming the victim and revisiting the horrific details of violent trauma. A blanket position of "it's not your (or the victim's) fault," without the stance of openness and inquisitiveness to the client's perceptions and experience, may result in the client feeling that important aspects of his traumatic reaction cannot be accepted and addressed.

PROFOUND CHANGE IN WORLDVIEW

Surviving family members tend to experience disturbing changes in some of their fundamental beliefs and assumptions. At the center of this change is an intense realization of their own fragility and vulnerability. The idea that bad things can happen to me, and that the world is dangerous become salient at a deeply felt level. Janoff-Bulman (1992) characterizes the essence of trauma as a "cornered horror." She observes that "Suddenly the victim's inner world is pervaded by thoughts and images representing malevolence, meaninglessness, and self-abasement. They are face to face with a dangerous universe, made all the more frightening by their total lack of psychological preparation" (p.63).

Survivors are profoundly changed by their experience. Part of their struggle is to reconstruct their sense of self and worldviews in ways that reflect an acknowledgment of the meaning of murder in their lives. To do so, they must integrate their deepened awareness of vulnerability, danger, and willful malevolence into a transformed personal experiential philosophy (Schillace, 2000).

Counseling offers a supportive venue for this process, particularly once the early crises and traumatic distress have diminished. The structure of counseling, with its encouragement of self-exploration and the creation of personal meaning, can greatly facilitate this reconstruction of self and worldview. The challenge for the counselor has more to do with attitude than technique. In short, the counselor needs to appreciate that this integration work is a vital part of the healing process, even though it is not directly concerned with symptom reduction or emotional disturbance. If insurance or the policy of the counseling setting dictate abbreviated counseling, it is important to refer the client to a setting (e.g., support group, minister, other counseling resources) that will support the client in the work discussed here.

Although this work is not technique driven, there are steps a counselor can take to facilitate this process. One is to inquire directly as to the client's feelings and views regarding such issues as trust and vulnerability, the limits of personal control and efficacy, the relationship of danger and safety, the belief that things will generally turn out well, what is particularly important to her in life, and the interplay of goodness and malevolence in life. A second step is to be responsive to their more complicated views as they come to an understanding of life that has goodness and trauma woven into its fabric. As Janoff-Bulman (1992) observes: "Survivors are often guardedly optimistic, but the rosy absolutism of earlier days is gone" (p. 174).

THE QUESTION OF CLOSURE

A common viewpoint in contemporary society is that survivor-victims need to gain closure. Closure is defined in the Random House Dictionary (1980) as "a conclusion or an end." Appealing though it may be, this goal is a fantasy. A critical counseling task is to help clients clarify what "working through" the murder experience means.

Essentially, it means that the sense of traumatic loss is no longer psychologically dominant in one's daily life. The client is able to trust and hope, albeit in a more careful way, make memories of the deceased, reengage with the community and move forward in a productive manner. Although no longer dominant, the survivor-victim's experience of the family member's murder is not over. One continues to relive and process the trauma and to grieve the loss, although usually in lower keys of intensity. Various events (e.g., anniversary of the death date, wedding of a family member or news story of a murder) may carry special meaning, intensify one's reactions and bring them more to consciousness for a time. Clients sometimes imagine that an event, such as the successful conclusion of a trial of the murderer, will bring closure. While they discover that such an event does lessen their traumatic distress, the story of the murder still remains alive in them.

"Working through" means arriving at some acknowledgment that this murder, in all its meanings, is part of one's self and one has been changed by it. Although no longer dominant, one lives around this experience and through it. It also means coming to terms with the reality that there are no answers for such a profound event. Why did this happen? Why did the murderer cross the boundaries into such extreme and physical cruelty, amorality and hatred? Ultimately, the survivor is left with a sense of mystery and chaos. What the police refer to as "motive" is not what the survivor means – and seeks to understand – by "motivation."

Many survivors struggle with questions of acceptance and forgiveness. The answers they arrive at are highly individual. In my clinical experience, I do not find it helpful to hold out acceptance and forgiveness as a goal or stage. Clients decide, without me, whether these are meaningful goals. Many former clients - who have gone on to live with purpose, love and connection – have not forgiven the murderer, although their rage is greatly diminished. Similarly, they have accepted the inevitable reality of what happened, but it still remains profoundly wrong and dissonant for them.

What is the counselor's role regarding these issues of closure? Fundamentally, the counselor needs to be as open to and empathic with the client's experience as possible. The counselor's task is to be supportive of the client's process of discovery and creation of their personal meaning, clarifying the meaning and validating the integrity of this process. Counselors must be especially sensitive to personal values and be careful to not make them expectations, however subtle, for the client. Part of the challenge is to help clients learn to live with the incoherence of murder in their lives and the lack of closure. Clients often welcome open discussions of these issues, initiated by the counselor. They have often sensed these issues but found them difficult to verbalize. Many clients have found that reading and discussing the book, *When Bad Things Happen To Good People* (1983), is very helpful in giving words to their experience and normalizing it. Helping clients become involved with support groups, such as Parents of Murdered Children, also contributes in this way.

COUNTERTRANSFERENCE

Countertransference reactions can be stimulated in any counseling situation. There is a particularly high poten-

tial for such reactions in the work with survivors (Herman, 1997). The intense feelings of rage, terror, despair or helplessness experienced by murder survivors can be overwhelming and evocative for the counselor. As Herman (1997) notes, trauma is contagious and some degree of "vicarious traumatization" is often inevitable.

Given the overarching importance of safety and empathy in the counseling relationship with survivors, attending to countertransference reactions is critical. Overidentification with the client's experience leaves the counselor vulnerable to taking actions that blur the boundaries and disempower the client, or result in a self-protective emotional withdrawal. Either situation will be disruptive to the working alliance and will reinforce the client's sense of stigma, isolation, shame, and fear.

Consequently, it is vital for the counselor to seek out supervision and consultation periodically. Also, it can be very beneficial to be a member of a peer support group. In both settings, it is important to be able to share one's emotional experience and receive strategic and intellectual guidance regarding one's work.

CONCLUSION

This chapter covers issues that are special to survivor-victims of a murdered family member. Trauma-specific interventions have presented for some of these issues. A second focus has been on perspective: both the challenge for the counselor in developing and maintaining an empathic perspective, and the client's need to gain perspective on the meaning of the traumatic experience and the changes in self and worldview that it triggers. The study of murder survivor-victims is in its infancy. Clinically oriented research will enhance work in this area.

References

Bard, M., & Sangrey, D. (1986). *The crime victim's handbook.* New York: Brunner/Mazel.

Herman, J. (1997). *Trauma and recovery.* New York: Basic Books.

James, B. (1988). *Treating traumatized children.* Lexington, MA: Lexington Books.

Janoff-Bulman, R. (1992). *Shattered assumptions: Towards a new psychology of trauma.* New York: Free Press.

Kushner, H.S. (1983). *When bad things happen to good people.* New York: Avon Books.

Meichenbaum, D. (1994). *A clinical handbook/practical therapist manual for assessing and treating adults with post-traumatic stress disorder.* Waterloo, Canada: Institute Press.

Rynearson, E.K. (2001). *Retelling violent death.* Philadelphia, PA: Brunner-Routledge.

Schillace, R. (2000). *Relationship pain.* New York: Writers Book Club.

Steele, W. (1997). *Trauma response kit: Short term trauma intervention.* Grosse Pointe Woods, MI: The Institute for Trauma and Loss in Children.

Stein, J. (Ed.) (1980). *The Random House dictionary.* New York: Ballantine Books.

Robert S. Fink, PhD, is an Associate Professor of Counseling, Oakland University, Rochester Hills, MI and is a psychologist in private practice.

Jill Riethmayer

Trauma invades the lives of individuals these days with much more frequency and by measures that are far more terrifying and destructive than in the past – more terrifying not only for children, but for adults as well. Adults and children of all ages feel the deep fear and anxiety that follows in the wake of a major trauma. In today's society, no one is truly "safe." It is as if trauma has mutated into a more powerful, invasive, and destructive strain than has existed in the past. One only has to remember September 11th, Oklahoma City, or Columbine to be reminded of the tragic impact trauma has upon both adults and children. What do individuals need after experiencing a major trauma, and how might counselors assist clients in getting those needs met after a traumatic event?

Trauma's initial impact brings four very powerful messages to a trauma survivor. It tells the survivor that the world is no longer a safe world, no longer a kind world, no longer a predictable world, and no longer a trustworthy world. Each of these has been taken away, or at least violated through the traumatic experience. Trauma, by its very definition, is unpredictable, dangerous, and destructive. For children, the loss of these four particular elements is even more devastating than for adults. Trauma literally robs children of a right to innocence that belongs to all children. This innocence, as in the case of sexual rape, is taken against a person's will and can never again be regained. The child's "world" is never again the same. The counselor can begin to meet these immediate needs of a trauma survivor by creating a counseling environment with the client that is safe, kind, predictable, and trustworthy. In some small way, a new therapeutic "world" is created that once again has characteristics of the client's world prior to the destructive trauma. Key in creating this counseling environment is the personification of these qualities by the therapist. Without these qualities,

a counseling relationship with a trauma survivor will not be effective; they are critical for success.

Trauma also brings three unwelcome effects into the life of the survivor. The first unwelcome effect is that of silence. Even when the initial shock of the trauma has begun to wane, the trauma survivor believes there are truly no words that can adequately describe the trauma that has been experienced. The second unwelcome element that enters the life of a trauma survivor is a sense of isolation. The survivor truly believes that no one could understand the depth of the terror that has been experienced and survived. The last unwelcome effect following a trauma is a sense of helplessness. At the time, nothing could be done to prevent or stop the trauma.

What does the counselor need to offer in helping the client work through these three unwelcome effects? First, the counselor assists the client in breaking the silence by gently guiding the client in finding words to describe the actual experience, as well as express the terror, pain, and sadness that accompanied the trauma. Next, the counselor helps to lessen the sense of isolation by joining the client in this emotional journey, and walking beside the client through the depths of the trauma work. Last, the counselor addresses the element of a sense of helplessness by continually encouraging and empowering the client to make the difficult journey through the trauma work in order to begin once again living life, instead of becoming overly focused and perhaps fixated on the past trauma. In this final phase, the counselor must empower the client to walk through the pain of the past trauma in order to emerge on the other side, ready to reach toward and fully grasp the future.

Trauma shatters the world of the survivor; what used to be "normal" no longer exists. In actuality, the world that existed prior to the trauma can never truly exist again. What must be done in trauma work is to reconstruct a new world—a "new normal." A major portion of the trauma work involves assisting the client in first identifying the remaining pieces following the shattering and then assisting the client in picking up those pieces. These pieces are often multifaceted—physical, emotional, financial, sexual, as well as spiritual.

The next portion of the counseling process is assisting the client to arrange (and rearrange) those remaining pieces in an attempt to make some kind of sense and meaning from the trauma. This does not imply that the counselor is going to make sense of a senseless trauma such as September 11th. However, it does mean that the counselor assists the client in finding some kind of greater meaning in the event. Often finding this meaning results in proactive efforts such as the creation of the organization MADD (Mothers Against Drunk Driving). In 1980, MADD was established by a group of women in California, outraged after the death of a teenage girl killed by a repeat-offender drunk driver.

Finally, the counselor must assist the client in defining a new normal. Life must be redefined not by what used to be, but by what now exists. A tool that helps to illustrate this shattering and reconstruction is a puzzle (an Adam's cube) that has six different colored and different shaped plastic pieces that can be arranged into a different shape for each of the six sides of the cube. Even though the six pieces do fit into all six sides of the cube, each side creates a different shape—a triangle, a square, an octagon, etc. When a client rearranges the remaining "pieces" following the shattering of a trauma, the client's life is never again identical to what it was prior to the trauma.

Trauma consistently brings a series of questions that the client must ask, and then the client must begin to search for answers. The counselor should be prepared for these questions as well as have a beginning response to assist the client in finding his or her own answers to the questions. Trauma survivors frequently ask the following questions:

- *Who (or what) else will I lose?*
  Helpful response: "Trauma is an event that is unusual—out of the ordinary. This exact trauma will probably not repeat itself."
- *Will I die?*
  Helpful response: "Eventually everyone dies, but unless you are sick or have an accident, death is probably not an immediate issue."

- *Am I loveable?*
  Helpful response: "Yes, you are very loveable." Remember that individuals (especially children) believe that bad things only happen to bad people. The response to this question should explore the truth of that belief.
- *Was it my fault?*
  Helpful response: "What do you think?" If the client did have some role in the cause of the trauma, do not address this issue until the client has first asked the question. The goal should then be to assist the client in owning his or her part in order to grieve and heal. Also be aware of magical thinking with children. A child often believes something happened because he or she wished that it would happen.
- *Could I have stopped it?*
  Helpful response: "Tell me how you could have stopped it." Assist the client in exploring whether he or she had the power, ability, or opportunity, etc. to stop the trauma.
- *Will I ever feel normal again?*
  Helpful response: "Yes, but normal won't feel like what normal used to feel like." Remind the client that it will be a *new* normal.
- *Am I going crazy?*
  Helpful response: "No, you are having a perfectly normal reaction to an out of the ordinary event."
- *How could God let this happen?*
  Helpful response: "I don't know. Tell me what you think about where God is in the midst of this trauma."
- *Will I ever laugh, (love), (trust) again?*
  Helpful response: "Yes, but probably not for quite a while. First, you will need to grieve your loss. Eventually you will be able to laugh, love, and trust again."

A large majority of the trauma work is grief work. This part involves working through the losses that the trauma has brought. In regard to the stages of grief, it is helpful to remember the following. Although the stages are listed in a specific order, a client will work (and rework) the stages in the unique order of his or her own grief journey. No two journeys through grief are the same—not even for two individuals experiencing the same exact loss. It is equally important to remember that each stage will be worked through in bits and pieces. Not all of the anger work will be done when a client is first in the anger stage. This stage, as well as the others, will be revisited as often as necessary by the client. Each time the stage is revisited, another portion of the anger work is done.

A major question that is often asked in the grieving process is how long the grieving process will take. Although this will vary for each individual client, there are four factors that will affect the length of the grieving process. The first factor is how close the person was to the individual who was lost. Of course, the closer the relationship, the longer the grieving process. The second factor having an impact on the length of the grieving process is how unexpected the loss was. (It is this factor that made the terrorists' attacks of September 11th so difficult.) The third factor that will have an impact on the grieving process is the role models that the person has had in his or her life. Has the client had the opportunity to see and learn a healthy grieving process, or has the client been denied that experience? The last factor applies to children. How old the child is at the time of the loss will have a bearing on both the manner in which the child grieves as well as the length of time the child grieves. All of these individual factors together will determine the approximate length of time that a client will need to grieve the trauma, along with its losses. Remember, grief takes as long as it takes!

Often, a counselor wonders how he or she will know when the trauma work has been completed. Basically, there are four major tasks in successful trauma or grief work. When these tasks have been completed successfully, the majority of the work has been completed. The first major task to be completed is that the survivor has finally accepted the reality of the loss or losses. This occurs when the losses have been identified and acknowledged, and the griever is no longer in denial or attempting to "bargain" with God, man, etc. in order to avoid the painful reality (and permanency) of the loss. The second major task is for the survivor to experience the pain of grief. This involves all the feeling work—accessing and feeling the pain, anger, sadness, and guilt about the loss. It includes exploring memories of the lost object or person as well as reviewing the important shared experiences of the past. In this phase, the important future hopes, dreams, and events that were to be shared with this person must also be grieved—for those will never be shared. The third task is adjusting to an environment without the lost object or person. The two major parts of this phase are learning to make some kind of "sense" out of the trauma and loss, while attempting some understanding of it, as well as accepting the finality of the loss. The final

task is when the survivor begins to resume normal activities and form new relationships to help fill the void created by the trauma and its subsequent losses. The energy that once went into grieving the past events and losses is now invested in the future. This indicates a critical turning point for the client. The client has moved the focus from the past to the present and is now ready to focus on the future.

What becomes crucial in the life of individuals who have been traumatized is not the magnitude of the trauma itself, but more importantly, who they have become in relationship to that pain. As Doris Stanford states in the introduction of her book, *Love Letters: Responding to Children in Pain*, "the same water that hardens an egg softens a carrot." It is the response to the trauma that determines the life-long impact the trauma has upon the trauma survivor. It is not the nature of the trauma that is critical to recovery, it is the individual's response to the trauma. What is vital is that the survivor does not become a hostage to the past; in essence, a hostage to the trauma itself. It is often the counselor and the support provided by the counselor that makes this critical difference in the life of a trauma survivor. This difference is often the difference between having a "past" and having a "future."

Finally, the helper must remember two key factors in relation to the work involved in healing from a trauma. First, the healing process will always take much longer than originally anticipated, and second, it will probably be far more difficult than expected. It is imperative for the helper to keep this in mind as the healing process evolves; otherwise it will be tempting to give up too easily or become impatient in the healing journey.

Does the hole torn into an individual's heart by trauma ever heal completely? No, not completely, but it does become smaller (and more bearable) through time and appropriate therapeutic intervention. What is critical to the individual's recovery is that there is an equipped professional who is willing to walk together with the client through the deep emotional pain of trauma in order to emerge victoriously on the other side of the trauma.

Jill Riethmayer, LPC, NCC, LMFT is Director of The Center for Student Assistance at Blinn College in Bryan, Texas.

Anne M. Brainerd

On Tuesday, September 11th, 2001, our nation was visited by evil. The tragic events of that day have caused immeasurable direct suffering for thousands of families, but the truth is that every American was affected by those events as if we all had been individually attacked.

You have undoubtedly said, and heard friends say, a variety of words to attempt to describe the feelings of the aftermath of this horror—confusion, frustration, fear, chaos, anger, depression, emptiness. Yet, even together those words don't fully describe what most of us are feeling.

As a nation we have been traumatized, and as an individual you have been traumatized. Don't think that because you weren't on one of the planes or in one of the buildings, or didn't have family or friends in those places, that you weren't affected. Our lives as Americans, and each of us personally, have been irrevocably altered.

You may now be experiencing powerful physical and emotional reactions. That's not unusual. Such reactions are normal, indeed healthy. It's your body and your mind responding to the aftershock. Physically, you may experience chills, fatigue, nausea, vomiting, or dizziness. You may experience confusion, nightmares, or poor concentration, or simply find it difficult to relax.

Emotionally, you may be feeling fear, guilt, grief, or nervousness. You may find yourself more irritable or prone to anger, or having sudden emotional outbursts. You are responding normally, in the way that we as feeling, thinking human beings are supposed to respond in the face of events too large and horrific for normal comprehension.

The problems that can arise are not in the emotions we feel, but in the ways we choose to respond to those emotions. Many people respond with denial, plunging themselves into their work. Some respond with drugs or alcohol, using them as a place to hide. Such responses can be harmful because they only numb you and don't validate your very real, very normal feelings.

A good starting point in responding to the feelings trauma generates is to go back to basics. Set up a schedule and stick to it. Get plenty of rest. Eat well-balanced, healthy meals, even if you don't feel hungry. Stay away from alcohol and drugs, which only dull the pain temporarily. Alternate exercise and relaxation, even if you feel like neither.

Try pampering yourself a little—take a hot bath, listen to your favorite music, read a beloved novel, allow yourself to cry. Most importantly, spend time with and talk with others. We've all been traumatized and we can all provide support for one another. You'll find most people willing and anxious to discuss their feelings and to listen to you explain yours.

Once your body, mind and emotions begin returning to a more normal state, you may still feel a void or a sense of inadequacy that you "haven't helped." If that is the case, look to your heart and to your own unique talents.

Perhaps you have the time to do some volunteer work. If so, do it locally. Many agencies would be grateful for your time, talents, dedication and smile. What you offer need not be tied to the tragedy in order for it to help you feel better. Pitching in to help on any worthwhile project will often reward you with substantial benefits.

Or you may find that your emotional needs can be met with personal acts. Perhaps you are a gardener. If so, plant a tree or a bed of flowers of remembrance. You'll pay tribute to those lost and give life and beauty back to America. Give blood. Even when not needed by the victims of the tragedy, it still is needed to save lives. Make a financial donation, if you can. Write a letter of support and thanks to the rescue workers. Visit someone in a hospital or nursing home who may be feeling forgotten at a time like this. Search for your unique gift or talent, and use it to the glory of our country and to the honor of our fallen.

Do not hide from the feelings that come to all of us in the light of such terrible events. Acknowledge what you are feeling, recognize that such feelings are normal, and then take positive steps to turn such feelings and emotions into positive actions that will help you feel better and help make this a better world.

Anne M. Brainerd is a graduate of the University of Southern Mississippi and has trained in crisis response with the International Critical Incident Stress Foundation.

ACA's *The Counseling Corner* is a weekly column carried by almost 300 newspapers nationwide, offering practical advice on variety of common problems.

Sharlene Hill

Family relationships are often under a great deal of stress. Balancing work, school, and other activities can take a real toll on both parents and children. Outside events, such as the tragic happenings of September 11th, can also be an unrealized source of tension and anxiety.

If we aren't careful, all these strains can result in weakened relationships within the family. Too often we put family time on the back burner, as we juggle the many activities packed into our daily schedules. Problems can begin to develop unnoticed and soon a family has grown apart. Yet there are simple ways to strengthen family ties and avoid such problems.

One simple and effective way to keep on top of a family's "growing pains" is to hold family meetings. Hold them often enough to work out everyday hassles (such as chores, errands, schedules, etc.). Typically, twice a month is enough, although this may be adjusted according to each family's needs. Regular meetings allow rules to be established and modified, activities planned and scheduled, and problems worked out. Family meetings can be fun, keep the family connected, and eliminate problems and keep a family running smoothly.

Before you begin holding meetings, decide on the ground rules. These can include requiring attendance by everyone, having only one person speak at a time, no yelling, name-calling, accusing or blaming, and having everyone make an effort to give helpful solutions.

Be creative when introducing the idea of regular meetings to your family. Maybe give them a special name, such as calling it a "family campfire." Hold your meetings someplace that is comfortable and free of distractions—maybe in a circle in the backyard or in the living room. Include a special treat as part of the meeting. Avoid chaos with fun gimmicks, such as having an object, maybe a small teddy bear, that gives the person holding it the right to talk, while the others remain silent until the object reaches them.

Begin family meetings on a positive note. Have each person share one exciting or special thing that happened to them since the last meeting. Next, allow each member to share one complaint or concern they have. Once a problem is aired, other members can give possible solutions when it's their turn to speak. Draw from these suggestions or use a combination of them to help solve the problems presented. Continue to discuss other family business in this manner. Have meetings end with each person sharing one thing they appreciate about the other family members or thanking other members for something said or done since the last meeting.

Another way to strengthen family ties is having a real family dinner once a week. Everyone should participate in preparing the meal and contribute to setting the table in a special way (candles, flowers, a child's handmade place setting or other art, etc.). Turn off the television and don't answer the phone. Make this a time to share positive stories. Avoid discussing problems and sensitive issues.

A family game night is another fun and inexpensive way to connect with each other. Make popcorn or other fun snacks and enjoy each others' company for the evening. Alternate which games are played, so everyone has the chance to play his or her favorite game. Again, turn off the television and don't answer the phone!

Family ties can also be improved through more personal attention. Set aside a few minutes each day, or an hour once a week, for one-on-one time with your children and your mate. It may seem hard to find the time, but with a little planning everyone can have a special time to give and receive undivided attention. One-on-one time with your mate is extremely important and should be at the top of your priority list. A strong relationship with your partner will provide a good role model for your children and aid in keeping a strong family bond.

In today's busy and often stressful world, staying connected with our mates and children is often not an easy task. Yet with simple efforts, it can be done and the benefits it can pay are enormous. Our mates and children should be the most important people in our lives and the source of a great deal of happiness. It's worth working at family ties to ensure that we are enjoying our family members and getting the most from those relationships.

Sharlene Hill is a graduate student in the Marriage and Family Counseling program at the University of Nevada, Reno.

ACA's *The Counseling Corner* is a weekly column carried by almost 300 newspapers nationwide, offering practical advice on a variety of common problems.

The American Counseling Association is the nation's largest organization of counseling professionals, with more than 50,000 members nationwide. Information for consumers and professional counselors is available through the ACA web site at www.counseling.org

National Mental Health Association

A disaster of any size will cause unusual stress in people who have been directly and indirectly impacted by it. Each person will react differently and a range of responses to a disaster are normal and to be expected. Emotional responses to disasters can appear immediately or sometimes months later.

The terrorist attacks in New York and Washington have had a profound impact on all Americans nationwide. Understanding what you're feeling and taking positive steps can help you cope with this disaster. Here are some common responses to disasters:

- Disbelief and shock
- Fear and anxiety about the future
- Disorientation, apathy and emotional numbing
- Irritability and anger
- Sadness and depression
- Feeling powerless
- Extreme hunger or lack of appetite
- Difficulty making decisions
- Crying for "no apparent reason"
- Headaches and stomach problems
- Difficulty sleeping
- Excessive drinking or drug use

Most of these reactions will decrease as time passes and you focus attention on daily activities. Because everyone experiences stress differently, don't compare your progress with others around you or judge other people's reactions and emotions.

WHAT YOU CAN DO

- Talk about it. Not expressing your feelings will keep you from being able to work through what happened. By talking with others, you will relieve stress and realize that other people share your feelings.
- Get plenty of rest and exercise. Remember to eat well. Avoid excessive drinking and risk-taking activities.
- Spend time with your family. If you have any children, encourage them to discuss their concerns and feelings with you.
- As soon as it feels comfortable, go back to your usual routine.
- Do things that you find relaxing and soothing.
- Recall other times you have experienced strong emotions and how they were resolved.
- Do something positive that will help you gain a greater sense of control (for example, give blood, take a first aid class or donate food or clothing).
- If you feel overwhelmed by the disaster, ask for help. It's not a sign of weakness. Talk with a trusted relative, friend, social worker, or clergy member.

If you have strong feelings that won't go away or if you are troubled for longer than four to six weeks, you may want to seek professional help. People who have existing mental health problems and those who have survived past trauma may also want to check in with a mental health care professional. Being unable to manage your responses to the disaster and resume your regular activities may be symptoms of post-traumatic stress disorder (PTSD), a real and treatable illness. Help is available.

National Mental Health Association
1021 Prince Street
Alexandria, VA 22314-2971
Phone 703/684-7722
Fax 703/684-5968

Copyrighted and published by the National Mental Health Association. Reprinted with permission. No part of this document may be produced without written consent.

National Mental Health Association

The terrorist attacks in New York City and Washington, D.C., have had a profound effect on people of all generations across the country. Although everyone responds to such tragedy with varying degrees of grief, fear and anger, many older adults who have lived through previous tragedies and trauma may be at greater risk for experiencing symptoms of post-traumatic stress disorder, depression or anxiety.

Some Common Responses to Disaster
- Disbelief and shock
- Fear and anxiety about the future
- Disorientation, apathy and emotional numbing
- Irritability and anger
- Sadness and depression
- Feeling powerless
- Over- or under-eating
- Difficulty making decisions
- Crying for "no apparent reason"
- Headaches and stomach problems
- Difficulty sleeping
- Excessive alcohol or drug use

You may experience all or only a few of these responses. Over time, these symptoms and difficulties should begin to decrease, as you refocus attention on your daily activities. However, everyone experiences stress differently so don't compare your progress with other people's or judge their reactions and emotions.

HOW TO COPE IN THE AFTERMATH
OF THE ATTACKS
- Talk about the experience and how you are feeling. Expressing your thoughts with others gives you the opportunity to relieve stress, reduce anxiety and realize that other people share your feelings.

- Communicate with loved ones often. Communicating with family and friends following a disaster helps increase feelings of safety and security.
- Take care of yourself physically. If exercise is a regular part of your routine, continue to exercise. It is also important to eat well, drink plenty of water and rest.
- Be around others. Isolation and loneliness can increase the degree to which you experience symptoms. If you do not have a local network of family or friends to visit with often, find a place where you can be with people. Volunteer at a local nonprofit, offer to speak at local schools about historical events you have experienced, contact local churches or senior centers to see if they are holding any activities of interest to you, or call your doctor or local mental health center to see if there is an older adults support group in your area that you could attend. If you are unable to drive, do not hesitate to ask for a ride, look into reduced special taxi fares for senior citizens, or take public transportation, if you are able.
- Do things you enjoy. If you have put things aside that you normally enjoy, get involved in those activities now. Go for that walk, plant flowers or play cards with your friends.
- Write about significant experiences in your life and how they have affected you. Journaling gives you the opportunity to express your feelings in your own words and at your own pace. It is also an opportunity for you to share pieces of your life with future generations.

It is important to return to your usual routine at your own pace; however, if your symptoms do not seem to be subsiding or if they appear to be getting worse, you

COPING WITH DISASTER. TIPS FOR OLDER ADULTS

may want to speak with a mental health professional. If you have already been diagnosed with a mental health disorder or if you find you are distressed about traumatic events from your past, you may want to meet with a mental health professional as a precautionary measure. To find a mental health professional in your community, contact your primary care physician, a local mental health center or your area Mental Health Association.

The National Mental Health Association (NMHA) has several resources available to help you and others cope with the disaster including Talking with Kids, Helping Your Workforce Cope and Return to Work, and fact sheets on post-traumatic stress disorder, depression, coping with loss and other topics. To obtain this information, visit www.nmha.org or call our toll-free line 800-969-NMHA (6642).

Copyrighted and published by the National Mental Health Association. Reprinted with permission. No part of this document may be produced without written consent.

National Mental Health Association
1021 Prince Street
Alexandria, VA 22314-2971
Phone 703/684-7722
Fax 703/684-5968

COPING WITH DISASTER WITHIN THE FAITH COMMUNITY

*American Association of Pastoral Counselors
and National Mental Health Association*

In the aftermath of the terrorist attacks, Americans of every religious and spiritual tradition are experiencing disbelief, grief, fear and even anger. Some may have lost family members, friends or work colleagues. Others have anxieties about the future. Nobody is unaffected.

The National Mental Health Association and the American Association of Pastoral Counselors have developed this fact sheet to assist people of faith and their communities in coping with the emotional and spiritual impact of our nation's tragedy.

Each person reacts differently to a disaster and a range of responses are normal and to be expected. Emotional responses to disasters can appear immediately or sometimes develop months later. Below is a list of common emotional and physical responses to disaster:

- Disbelief and shock
- Disorientation; difficulty making decisions or concentrating
- Apathy and emotional numbing
- Sadness and depression
- Fear and anxiety about the future
- Intrusive thoughts; replaying events in our minds
- Excessive worry about safety and vulnerability; feeling powerless
- Irritability and anger
- Headaches and stomach problems
- Difficulty sleeping
- Extreme changes in eating patterns; loss of appetite or overeating
- Excessive use of alcohol and drugs

For many, the tragic events not only challenge the emotional and physical sense of well being, but also one's spirituality. People want to find some meaning in the tragedies and come to grips with our nation's response. As a result, many Americans are turning to their faith through prayer and meditation to try to cope with their feelings and seek support, reassurance and understanding during this time of crisis.

While some people find turning to their faith helpful, others may be troubled by questions and doubts. They may have difficulty sorting out the ambiguities of life and faith. Questions and doubts at this difficult time are normal. What's important to remember is that trust, hope and strength are perhaps the most essential elements of all faiths.

TIPS FOR PEOPLE OF FAITH

Places of worship can be supportive environments for individuals. Here are some ideas on finding ways to cope within your faith community:

Connect: Spend additional time with family, friends and members of your house of worship. Reach out to others for assurance and support. We need to love and be loved. Connect with those you love and emphasize the importance of relationships. Draw strength from your faith.

Communicate: Recognize the importance of talking about what happened. By talking with others, you will relieve stress and realize that other people experience similar reactions. Share your feelings with your priest, minister, rabbi, imam, or other clergy. Parents should encourage children to discuss their concerns and feelings.

Act: Find activities that are positive for your spirit, mind and body. Consider doing things that contribute to others. Be intentional with your time and do things that impact positively on your life. Candlelight vigils and prayer groups are good ways to encourage togetherness and reassurance within the faith community. You may also want to help organize volunteer services such as food banks, clothing collections and blood drives.

Get Help: For most people, the negative feelings will decrease as time passes, but some may have difficulty coping with their feelings or resuming regular activities.

If you have strong feelings that won't go away or are troubled for longer than four to six weeks, you may want to seek professional help. People who have existing mental health problems and those who have survived past trauma may also want to check in with a mental health care professional.

For people of faith, pastoral counselors are a resource in helping to address both mental health and spiritual concerns. If you would like to contact a Certified Pastoral Counselor in your area, call the American Association of Pastoral Counselors Referral Service at 800-225-5603 or visit www.aapc.org.

The National Mental Health Association has several resources available to help you and others cope with the disaster, including Time for Reassurance, Talking with Kids, Coping Tips for Adults and fact sheets on post-traumatic stress, depression, coping with loss and other topics. To obtain this information, go to www.nmha.org or call our toll-free line 800-969-NMHA (6642).

Reprinted with permission.

Flagstaff Child and Family Counseling Center

Although trauma affects people differently, there are some common reactions that you may experience. These signs and symptoms may begin immediately, or you may feel fine for a couple of days or even weeks, then suddenly be hit with a reaction. The important thing to remember is that these reactions are quite normal; although you may feel some distress, you're probably experiencing a normal reaction to abnormal situation. Some common responses to traumatic events are:

Physical reactions:
• Insomnia/nightmares
• Fatigue
• Hyperactivity or "nervous energy"
• Appetite changes
• Pain in the neck or back
• Headaches
• Heart palpitations or pains in the chest
• Dizzy spells

Emotional reactions:
• Flashbacks or "reliving" the event
• Excessive jumpiness or tendency to be startled
• Irritability
• Anger
• Feelings of anxiety or helplessness

Effect on productivity:
• Inability to concentrate increased incidence of errors
• Lapses of memory
• Increase in absenteeism
• Tendency to overwork

Usually, the signs and symptoms of trauma will lessen with time. If you are concerned about your reaction, note the specific symptoms that worry you. For each symptom, note the:

Duration. Normally, trauma reactions will grow less intense and disappear within a few weeks.

Intensity. If the reaction interferes with your ability to carry on your life normally, you may wish to seek help. If you are concerned that your trauma response is too intense, or is lasting too long, please seek counseling. Your EAP, community mental health center, physician or priest, minister or rabbi may be able to refer you to a qualified counselor. Whether you choose to seek counseling or not, the following tips can help you keep your life in order while you experience the trauma response:

• Maintain as normal a schedule as possible, but don't overdo it. Cut out unnecessary "busyness" and don't take on new projects.
• Acknowledge that you'll be operating below normal level for a while.
• Structure your time even more carefully than usual. It's normal to forget things when you're under stress. Keep lists, and double-check any important work.
• Maintain control where you can. Make small decisions, even if you feel that it's unimportant or you don't care. It's important to maintain control in some areas of your life.
• Spend time with others, even though it may be difficult at first. It's easy to withdraw when you're hurt, but now you need the company of others.
• Give yourself time. You may feel better for a while, then have a "relapse." This is normal. Allow plenty of time….

Prepared by the Flagstaff Child and Family Counseling Center, Flagstaff Arizona and the American Counseling Association (www.counseling.org/tragedy/responses.html).

American Counseling Association

Not surprisingly, the tragic events of September 11th brought strong emotional reactions from many children. As they hear their parents talk, pick up bits from TV and radio reports, and talk with friends, even young children can gain enough of an understanding of a crisis situation and the tension it has brought, to feel threatened, insecure and generally upset.

While every child will display emotional responses that differ in their nature and severity, there are some common emotions that occur in reaction to most crisis situations. Fear and anxiety are two of the most common. Children may assume that the bad things that have happened could also happen to them. They may also become anxious and uncertain because they know or understand only part of what is happening. Children also fear the loss of stability in their lives. They sense things have changed, but don't know what it really means for them.

In times of crisis, children need caring adults who are willing to help them understand and deal with the emotions they're facing. There are many things you can do to help your children at these times:

- Listen to your child. Encourage him or her to express what he or she is feeling. Let your child know you understand those feelings.
- Respond to questions honestly, but in an age-appropriate manner. A 6-year old does not need or want all the details; a 12-year old may feel even more threatened if it appears you are hiding things.
- Be willing to discuss difficult issues. You won't have all the answers, but be willing to talk about what you do know and understand. Encouraging your child to express his or her thoughts can help the child put the situation into perspective.
- Limit exposure to negative information for younger children (up to about age 9 or 10). Too many adult-oriented details (as from TV reports) will make most children, especially younger children, feel more anxious and emotional.
- Stick to factual information. Avoid projecting your own fears onto your child. Your children are sensitive to your feelings and will pick up on your emotional state. Be as strong and supportive as possible. It's okay to stress how serious a situation might be, but don't increase your child's fears of what is happening.
- Look for signs that your child may be having a strong emotional reaction, even if it isn't being verbally expressed. Crying, nightmares, or repeatedly asking the same anxious questions are signs of a strong emotional reaction. Subtle signs such as facial expressions, voice tone, mood swings and overall behavior also indicate how your child is feeling and reacting.
- Offer reassurances to a child of his or her safety. Crisis events often bring changes, such as increased security. Let your child know how such changes pertain to his or her personal safety.
- Assure your child you're personally there to protect and provide. Provide both verbal and physical reassurances of your love and your caring. Say "I love you" and offer hugs and kisses to back up that message.
- Accept that your child may have reactions he or she can't control—nightmares, behavior changes, emotional outbursts, anger. Don't blame your child for such reactions. Help him or her understand what is happening. Be there to comfort, support and help.
- Try to maintain normal routines. Helping the child to see that family life is still the same, despite the crisis, is reassuring. Adding some

123

special touches, such as an extra stuffed animal or extra story time for a young child, can help reduce nighttime anxieties.

• Discuss, but don't over-emphasize, your own feelings. Make it clear there's nothing wrong with feeling a little scared, upset, sad or confused. Discuss how to cope with and overcome such feelings.

• Be honest. Children usually know when they're being mislead. Don't make them more scared or insecure by having those they love and trust most not willing to tell them the truth.

If your child is having an especially strong reaction to the situation, seek professional help. Your school counselor is a good starting point. Your church or synagogue may also be able to offer assistance, or provide the names of counseling professionals trained to work with children. Your local mental health organization or mental health center can be another source for references.

ACA's *The Counseling Corner* is a weekly column carried by almost 300 newspapers nationwide, offering practical advice on a variety of common problems.

National Institute of Mental Health

Reactions to trauma may appear immediately after the traumatic event or days and even weeks later. Loss of trust in adults and fear of the event occurring again are responses seen in many children and adolescents who have been exposed to traumatic events. Other reactions vary according to age: (Footnotes 1-4)

For children 5 years of age and younger, typical reactions can include a fear of being separated from the parent, crying, whimpering, screaming, immobility and/or aimless motion, trembling, frightened facial expressions and excessive clinging. Parents may also notice children returning to behaviors exhibited at earlier ages (these are called regressive behaviors), such as thumb-sucking, bedwetting, and fear of darkness. Children in this age bracket tend to be strongly affected by the parents' reactions to the traumatic event.

Children 6 to 11 years old may show extreme withdrawal, disruptive behavior, and/or inability to pay attention. Regressive behaviors, nightmares, sleep problems, irrational fears, irritability, refusal to attend school, outbursts of anger and fighting are also common in traumatized children of this age. Also the child may complain of stomachaches or other bodily symptoms that have no medical basis. Schoolwork often suffers. Depression, anxiety, feelings of guilt and emotional numbing or "flatness" are often present as well.

Adolescents 12 to 17 years old may exhibit responses similar to those of adults, including flashbacks, nightmares, emotional numbing, avoidance of any reminders of the traumatic event, depression, substance abuse, problems with peers, and anti-social behavior. Also common are withdrawal and isolation, physical complaints, suicidal thoughts, school avoidance, academic decline, sleep disturbances, and confusion. The adolescent may feel extreme guilt over his or her failure to prevent injury or loss of life, and may harbor revenge fantasies that interfere with recovery from the trauma.

Some youngsters are more vulnerable to trauma than others, for reasons scientists don't fully understand. It has been shown that the impact of a traumatic event is likely to be greatest in the child or adolescent who previously has been the victim of child abuse or some other form of trauma, or who already had a mental health problem (Footnotes 5-8). And the youngster who lacks family support is more at risk for a poor recovery (Footnote 9).

1. Osofsky JD. The effects of exposure to violence on young children. American Psychologist, 1995; 50(9): 782-8.

2. Pynoos RS, Steinberg AM, Goenjian AK. Traumatic stress in childhood and adolescence: recent developments and current controversies. In: Van der Kolk BA, McFarlane AC, Weisaeth L, eds. Traumatic stress: the effects of overwhelming experience on mind, body, and society. New York: Guilford Press, 1996; 331-58.

3. Marans S, Adelman A. Experiencing violence in a developmental context. In: Osofsky JD, et al., eds. Children in a violent society. New York: Guilford Press, 1997; 202-22.

4. Vogel JM, Vernberg EM. Psychological responses of children to natural and human-made disasters: I. Children's psychological responses to disasters. Journal of Clinical Child Psychology, 1993; 22(4): 464-84.

5. Garbarino J, Kostelny K, Dubrow N. What children can tell us about living in danger. American Psychologist, 1991; 46(4): 376-83.

6. Duncan RD. Saunders BE, Kilpatrick DG, Hanson RF, Resnick HS. Childhood physical assault as a risk factor for PTSD, depression. and substance abuse: findings from a national survey. American Journal of Orthopsychiatry. 1996; 66(3): 437-48.

7. Boney-McCoy S. Finkelhor D. Prior victimization: a risk factor for child sexual abuse and for PTSD-related symptomatology among sexually abused youth. Child Abuse and Neglect, 1995; 19(12): 1401-21.

8. Roth SH, Newman E, Pelcovitz D, Van der Kolk BA, Mandel FS. Complex PTSD in victims exposed to sexual and physical abuse: results from the DSM-IV Field Trial for Posttraumatic Stress Disordcr. Journal of Traumatic Stress, 1997; 10(4): 539-55.

9. Morrison JA. Protective factors associated with children's emotional responses to chronic community violence exposure. Trauma, Violence, and Abuse: A Review Journal, 2000; 1(4); 299-320.

Reprinted with permission from ERIC Counseling and Student Services Clearinghouse and the National Institute of Mental Health.
http://www.nimh.nih.gov/publicat/violence.cfm

HELPING CHILDREN COPE WITH LOSS, DEATH AND GRIEF: RESPONSE TO A NATIONAL TRAGEDY

34

National Association Of School Psychologists

The security and safety that was a hallmark of our American society was shattered by the events of September 11th. Never before in our nation's history have so many lives been lost in a single day. Communities are impacted by multiple losses that stretch their capacities to cope. It is difficult to predict how students, adults and schools will be able to deal with the harsh realities of life in the coming weeks, months and years. Children who have experienced the loss of one or both parents, siblings, other relatives, friends, or neighbors are now suffering from profound grief. How can caring adults help these children deal with loss of this magnitude? How can we begin to understand and respond to the depths of their suffering? One thing we do know is that this will be an extremely difficult and painful task. Children and adolescents will need all the support they can get and they will require a long time to recover. Life may not be the same for anyone in this country, but those youngsters who have sustained personal losses may require significant assistance from trained, caring adults.

EXPRESSIONS OF GRIEF

Talking to children about death must be geared to their developmental level and their capacity to understand the related facts of the situation. Children will be aware of the reactions of significant adults as they interpret and react to information about death and tragedy. The range of reactions that children display in response to the death of significant others may include:

- Emotional shock and at times an apparent lack of feelings, which serve to help the child detach from the pain of the moment;
- Regressive (immature) behaviors, such as needing to be rocked or held, difficulty separating from parents or significant others, needing to

sleep in parent's bed or an apparent difficulty completing tasks well within the child's ability level;
- Explosive emotions and acting out behavior that reflect the child's internal feelings of anger, terror, frustration and helplessness. Acting out may reflect insecurity and a way to seek control over a situation for which they have little or no control;
- Asking the same questions over and over, not because they do not understand the facts, but rather because the information is so hard to believe or accept. Repeated questions can help listeners determine if the child is responding to misinformation or the real trauma of the event.

HELPING CHILDREN COPE

The following tips will help teachers and parents support children who have experienced the loss of parents or loved ones. Some of these recommendations come from Dr. Alan Wolfelt, Director of the Center for Loss and Life Transition in Fort Collins, Colorado.

- **Allow children to be the teachers about their grief experiences:** Give children the opportunity to tell their story and be a good listener.
- **Don't assume that every child in a certain age group understands death in the same way or with the same feelings:** All children are different and their view of the world is unique and shaped by different experiences. (Developmental information is provided below.)
- **Grieving is a process, not an event;** Parents and schools need to allow adequate time for each child to grieve in the manner that works for that child. Pressing children to resume "normal" activities without the chance to deal with their

emotional pain may prompt additional problems or negative reactions.

- **Don't lie or tell half-truths to children about the tragic event:** Children are often bright and sensitive. They will see through false information and wonder why you do not trust them with the truth. Lies do not help the child through the healing process or help develop effective coping strategies for life's future tragedies or losses.

- **Help all children, regardless of age, to understand loss and death:** Give the child information at the level that he/she can understand. Allow the child to guide adults as to the need for more information or clarification of the information presented. Loss and death are both part of the cycle of life that children need to understand.

- **Encourage children to ask questions about loss and death:** Adults need to be less anxious about not knowing all the answers. Treat questions with respect and a willingness to help the child find his or her own answers.

- **Don't assume that children always grieve in an orderly or predictable way:** We all grieve in different ways and there is no one "correct" way for people to move through the grieving process.

- **Let children know that you really want to understand what they are feeling or what they need.** Sometimes children are upset but they cannot tell you what will be helpful. Giving them the time and encouragement to share their feelings with you may enable them to sort out their feelings.

- **Children will need long-lasting support:** The more losses the child or adolescent suffered, the more difficult it will be to recover. This is especially true if they lost a parent who was their major source of support. Try to develop multiple supports for children who suffered significant losses.

- **Keep in mind that grief work is hard:** It is hard work for adults and hard for children as well.

- **Understand that grief work is complicated:** When death results from a terrorist act, this brings forth many issues that are difficult, if not impossible, to comprehend. Grieving will also be complicated by a need for vengeance or justice and by the lack of resolution of the current situation: Perpetrators may still be at large and our nation is at war. The sudden nature of death and the fact that many individuals were considered missing rather than dead further complicates the grieving process.

- **Be aware of your own need to grieve:** Focusing on the children in your care is important, but not at the expense of your emotional needs. Adults who have lost a loved one will be far more able to help children work through their grief if they get help themselves. For some families, it may be important to seek family grief counseling. as well as individual sources of support.

DEVELOPMENTAL PHASES IN UNDERSTANDING DEATH

It is important to recognize that all children are unique in their understanding of death and dying. This understanding depends on their developmental level, cognitive skills, personality characteristics, religious or spiritual beliefs, teachings by parents and significant others, input from the media, and previous experiences with death. Nonetheless, there are some general considerations that will be helpful in understanding how children and adolescents experience and deal with death.

- **Infants and Toddlers:** The youngest children may perceive that adults are sad, but have no real understanding of the meaning or significance of death.

- **Preschoolers:** Young children may deny death as a formal event and may see death as reversible. They may interpret death as a separation, not a permanent condition. Preschool and even early elementary children may link certain events and magical thinking with the causes of death. As a result of the World Trade Center disaster, some children may imagine that going into tall buildings may cause someone's death.

- **Early Elementary School:** Children at this age (approximately 5–9) start to comprehend the finality of death. They begin to understand that certain circumstances may result in death. They can see that, if large planes crash into buildings, people in the planes and buildings will be killed. However, they may over-generalize, particularly at ages 5–6—if jet planes don't fly, then people don't die. At this age, death is perceived as something that happens to others, not to oneself or one's family.

- **Middle School:** Children at this level have the cognitive understanding to comprehend death as a final event that results in the cessation of all bodily functions. They may not fully grasp the abstract concepts discussed by adults or on the

TV news but are likely to be guided in their thinking by a concrete understanding of justice. They may experience a variety of feelings and emotions, and their expressions may include acting out or self-injurious behaviors as a means of coping with their anger, vengeance and despair.

- **High School:** Most teens will fully grasp the meaning of death in circumstances such as the World Trade Center or Pentagon disasters. They may seek out friends and family for comfort or they may withdraw to deal with their grief. Teens (as well as some younger children) with a history of depression, suicidal behavior and chemical dependency are at particular risk for prolonged and serious grief reactions and may need more careful attention from home and school during these difficult times.

TIPS FOR CHILDREN AND TEENS WITH GRIEVING FRIENDS AND CLASSMATES

Many children and teens have been indirectly impacted by the terrorists' attacks. They have learned of the deaths of people close to their friends and classmates—parents, siblings, other relatives and neighbors. Particularly in areas near the World Trade Center or Pentagon, it is not unusual to find several children in a given classroom who lost a family member—or even multiple family members. Additionally, all over the country, children have been impacted by the death of a family member at either the attack site or on board one of the four hijacked planes. Seeing their friends try to cope with such loss may scare or upset children who have had little or no experience with death and grieving. Some suggestions teachers and parents can provide to children and youth to deal with this "secondary" loss:

- Particularly with younger children, it will be important to help clarify their understanding of death. See tips above under "helping children cope."
- Seeing their classmates reactions to loss may bring about some fears of losing their own parents or siblings. Children need reassurance from caretakers and teachers that their own families are safe. For children who have experienced their own loss (previous death of a parent, grandparent, sibling), observing the grief of a friend can bring back painful memories. These children are at greater risk for developing more serious stress reactions and should be given extra support as needed.

- Children (and many adults) need help in communicating condolence or comfort messages. Provide children with age-appropriate guidance for supporting their peers. Help them decide what to say (e.g., "Steve, I am so sorry about your father. I know you will miss him very much. Let me know if I can help you with your paper route...") and what to expect (see "expressions of grief" above).
- Help children anticipate some changes in friends' behavior. It is important that children understand that their grieving friends may act differently, may withdraw from their friends for a while, might seem angry or very sad, etc., but that this does not mean a lasting change in their relationship.
- Explain to children that their "regular" friendship may be an important source of support for friends and classmates. Even normal social activities such as inviting a friend over to play, going to the park, playing sports, watching a movie, or a trip to the mall may offer a much needed distraction and sense of connection and normalcy.
- Children need to have some options for providing support—it will help them deal with their fears and concerns if they have some concrete actions that they can take to help. Suggest making cards, drawings, helping with chores or homework, etc. Older teens might offer to help the family with some shopping, cleaning, errands, etc., or with babysitting for younger children.
- Encourage children who are worried about a friend to talk to a caring adult. This can help alleviate their own concern or potential sense of responsibility for making their friend feel better. Children may also share important information about a friend who is at risk of more serious grief reactions.
- Parents and teachers need to be alert to children in their care who may be reacting to a friend's loss of a loved one. These children will need some extra support to help them deal with the sense of frustration and helplessness that many people are feeling at this time.

RESOURCES FOR GRIEVING AND TRAUMATIZED CHILDREN

At times of severe stress, such as the trauma of the terrorist attacks on our country, both children and adults need extra support. Children closest to this tragedy may very well experience the most dramatic feelings of fear, anxiety and loss. They may have personally lost a loved one or know of friends and schoolmates who have been devastated by these treacherous acts. Adults need to carefully observe these children for signs of traumatic stress, depression or even suicidal thinking, and seek professional help when necessary.

Resources to help you identify symptoms of severe stress and grief reactions are available at the National Association of School Psychologists website—www.nasponline.org. See also:

For Caregivers:
Deaton, R.L., & Berkan, W.A. (1995). Planning and managing death issues in the schools: A handbook. Westport, CT: Greenwood Publishing Group.

Mister Rogers Website: www.misterrogers.org (see booklet on Grieving for children 4-10 years)

Webb, N.B. (1993). Helping bereaved children: A handbook for practitioners. New York: Guilford Press.

Wolfelt, A. (1983). Helping children cope with grief. Bristol, PA: Accelerated Development.

Wolfelt, A (1997). Healing the bereaved child: Grief gardening, growth through grief and other touchstones for caregivers. Ft. Collins, CO: Companion.

Worden, J.W. (1996). Children and grief: When a parent dies. New York: Guilford Press

For Children:
Gootman, M.E. (1994). When a friend dies: A book for teens about grieving and healing. Minneapolis: Free Spirit Publishing.

Greenlee, S. (1992). When someone dies. Atlanta: Peachtree Publishing. (Ages 9-12).

Wolfelt, A.(2001). Healing your grieving heart for kids. Ft. Collins, CO: Companion. (See also similar titles for teens and adults)

© 2001, National Association of School Psychologists

Reprinted with permission from ERIC Counseling and Student Services Clearinghouse, and the National Association of School Psychologists.

TRAUMA AND CHILDREN: A PARENT HANDOUT FOR HELPING CHILDREN HEAL

Philip J. Lazarus

Every parent at one time has worried about harm befalling their children. When trauma to children occurs, the territory of everyday life becomes frightening and unfamiliar not only for children but parents as well. Parents may find themselves overcome with anxiety and fear. Trauma may send a shockwave to the system and parents may respond with a wide range of feelings. These feelings may include a sense of disbelief, helplessness, isolation, despair, or horror. Parents may try to make sense out of a senseless act. Who can prepare for their children being physically or sexually assaulted, kidnapped, mugged, robbed or involved in a severe automobile accident? Who can prepare for children being diagnosed with a life threatening illness or experiencing a natural or man-made disaster?

Traumas typically occur suddenly, often leaving children little or no time to prepare physically or emotionally. Traumas are unpredictable and outside what is to be expected in children's lives. During a trauma, children experience intense fear, horror or helplessness. Typical methods of coping no longer work. Following trauma, children require extra support and need to learn new coping strategies.

Parents can be instrumental in their children's recovery. Therefore, helping children recover from a trauma is a family matter. Parents need to take the lead and model positive coping. Yet parents themselves may require extra information, support and resources to assist their children. Some first steps that parents can take are to understand the impact and symptoms of trauma and how to help in the aftermath. This handout provides this information.

THE IMPACT OF TRAUMA

Trauma can change the way children view their world. Assumptions about safety and security are now challenged. Children's reactions will depend upon the severity of the trauma, their personality makeup, their characteristic coping style and the availability of support. It is common for children to regress both behaviorally and academically following a trauma. A constructive way to view the situation is that they are normal children in an abnormal circumstance.

It is natural for children to first experience some sort of denial. For example, children may insist upon returning to a house that has been destroyed. Fears, worries or nightmares are common following a trauma. Sleep disturbances or eating difficulties may happen. Also children may begin to regress emotionally or act younger than their chronological age. They also may become more clinging, unhappy and needy of parental attention and comfort. Feelings of irritability, anger, sadness or guilt may often emerge. Somatic complaints such as headaches, stomachaches or sweating are not unusual. Some loss of interest in school and poor concentration are some other common reactions.

SYMPTOMS ASSOCIATED WITH POST TRAUMATIC STRESS DISORDER

Following a trauma, children may experience some of the symptoms of Post Traumatic Stress Disorder (PTSD). The main symptoms are as follows:

Re-experiencing of the trauma during play or dreams. For example, children may:

- Repeatedly act out what happened when playing with toys
- Have many distressing dreams about the trauma
- Be distressed when exposed to events that resemble the trauma or at the anniversary of the trauma event
- Act or feel as if the trauma is happening again

Avoidance of reminders of the trauma and general numbness to all emotional topics. For example, children may:

- Avoid all activities that remind them of the trauma
- Withdraw from other people
- Have difficulty feeling positive emotions

Increased "arousal" symptoms. For example, children may:

- Have difficulty failing or staying asleep
- Be irritable or quick to anger
- Have difficulty concentrating
- Startle more easily

WHAT CAN I DO AS A PARENT FOLLOWING A TRAUMA?

Establish a sense of safety and security. It is essential that children feel protected, safe and secure in the aftermath of a trauma. Ensure that all basic needs are met, including love, care and physical closeness. Spend extra time to let children know that someone will nurture and protect them. Children will need a lot of comforting and reassurance.

Listen actively to your children. Seek first to understand before trying to be understood. Parents may underestimate the extent of the trauma experienced by their children. It is often not as important what you say, but that you listen with empathy and patience. In some instances your children may be reluctant to initiate conversations about trauma. If so, it may be helpful to ask them what they think other children felt or thought about the event. Also, it may be easier for children to tell what happened (e.g., what they saw, heard, smelled, physically felt) before they can discuss their feelings about the trauma. In other instances, children will want to tell their parents the story of the trauma over and over. Retelling is part of the healing process. Children need to tell their stories and have their parents listen, again and again to each and every agonizing detail.

Help your children express all their emotions. It is important to talk to your children about the tragedy—to address the suddenness and irrationality of the disaster. Reenactment and play about the trauma should be encouraged. It is helpful to ensure that children have time to paint, draw or write about the event. Provide toys that may enable children to work through the trauma. Examples may include such items as a toy fire engine, ambulances, fire extinguisher, doctor kit, etc. for a girl injured in a fire.

Imagining alternate endings to the disaster may help empower your children and allow them to feel less helpless in the aftermath of a tragedy. Validate your children's feelings. Help children understand that following a trauma all feelings are acceptable. Children will probably experience a myriad of feelings which could include shame, rage, anger, sadness, guilt, pain, isolation, loneliness and fear. Help your children understand that what they are experiencing is normal and to be expected.

Allow your children the opportunity to regress as necessary. This is important so that they may "emotionally regroup." For example, your children may request to sleep in your bed with the lights on or you may need to drive your children to school. Previously developed skills may seem to disappear or deteriorate. Bedwetting or thumb sucking may occur. Aggression and anger may emerge in a previously non-aggressive child. Be patient and tolerant and never ridicule. Remember that most regression following a trauma is temporary.

Help children clear up misconceptions. Help correct misunderstandings regarding the cause or nature of the trauma, especially those that relate to inappropriate guilt, shame, embarrassment or fear. (Examples may be "I should have been able to save my brother from the car wreck." "God struck my sister dead because God was angry at her." "My father died of cancer and I will catch it from him.")

Educate yourself about trauma and crisis. The more you know about trauma, the more empowered you may feel. To help educate yourself, consider setting up a conference with the school psychologist or mental health professional in your school. A good place to start is by reading the text listed below under "Resource for Parents."

Help predict and prepare. If your children need to go to a funeral or deal with surgery, carefully explain what will happen each step of the way. Allow your children to ask all kinds of questions. If they need to appear in court, explain what they will see, hear, do, etc.

Arrange support for yourself and your family as necessary. Consult with your clergy, rabbi, physician and friends as necessary. You may need extra emotional, religious, medical and/or psychological support. If possible take appropriate time for recreational or pleasurable experiences with your children to establish a sense of normalcy and continuity.

Communicate with the school and staff about what occurred. Most teachers will be understanding and helpful if they know that children had a traumatic experience. Teachers may be able to provide additional support both educationally and emotionally. They can also provide information to doctors or therapists or alert you to troublesome behaviors they observe.

Affirm that your children are capable of coping and healing in the aftermath of' a trauma. Plant "emotional seeds" that express confidence in your children's ability to heal. Remember the messages that you give your children have incredible power.

Seek professional assistance for your children and family as necessary. When seeking help, make sure the professional has experience with children and has treated crisis and trauma. Feel free to discuss with the therapist all your concerns and all aspects of treatment. If your children are experiencing the symptoms of PTSD, then therapy may be warranted.

WHAT CAN I SAY AS A PARENT FOLLOWING A TRAUMA?

- Sometimes knowing exactly what to say is difficult. However, your emotional expression of love and concern is more important than words. Just saying "This is very hard for us" can lead to emotional relief and understanding.
- Always be honest with your children about what has happened and what may occur. Remember that following a trauma, children may lose a sense of trust about the safety and security of the world. Therefore, honesty is essential so your children can maintain a sense of trust.
- Respect your children's fears. Children cannot be helped by trying to argue them out of their fears by appeals to bravery or reason. What is most helpful is an approach that says "I know you are feeling frightened now." This can be followed by an offer of assistance and support by saying, "Let's see what we can do to make this less scary for you."
- Make sure that your children know that you are aware of the seriousness of the situation. Allow your children to cry. Saying to your children "Don't cry, everything will be fine" denies the seriousness of the situation.
- Try to recognize your children's feelings and put them into words. For example, if a child's close friend died in an automobile accident, you might say to your child "You are sad and angry that your friend was killed. I know that you must miss him very much." Or if a child feels overwhelmed by fears in the aftermath of a hurricane, you may say "I know that you are frightened, but we have a plan to protect us if another hurricane occurs."

WHAT SHOULD I DO IF I BELIEVE MY CHILD MAY BE SUFFERING FROM PTSD?

Consult with your local school psychologist or contact a mental health professional who has experience in this area such as a psychiatrist, psychologist or mental health counselor. Your school psychologist or pediatrician may direct you to the appropriate resources.

WHAT TYPE OF THERAPY IS RECOMMENDED FOR TRAUMATIZED CHILDREN?

A variety of methods may be used depending on the orientation of a particular therapist. Very different approaches to the same problem can be equally effective when undertaken by an insightful and skilled professional. Approaches may include individual, group or family therapy. Therapists often use play, art and drama methods in their treatment as well as "cognitive-behavioral" approaches, which help children reinterpret events and feelings in a more positive way, or in some cases they might use clinical hypnosis. As part of the therapy experience, children will be guided to reprocess the trauma in a safe and supportive environment. In some instances medication may be used to control severe anxiety, depression or sleeplessness. However, medication should not be used as a substitute for psychotherapy for traumatized children.

IF I SEEK THERAPEUTIC SERVICES FOR MY CHILDREN, WHAT WILL BE THE GOALS OF THERAPY?

The goals of therapy with traumatized children should include:

- Gaining a sense of mastery and control over one's life
- The safe expression and release of feelings
- Relief of painful symptoms and post traumatic behaviors
- Minimizing the scars of trauma
- Corrections of any misunderstandings and self-blame
- Restoration of hope regarding the future
- Establishing a renewed sense of trust in oneself and the world
- Developing perspective and distance regarding the trauma

Summary

Helping children recover from trauma is a family matter. It is important to maintain an open discussion of the trauma and recognize the feelings of all family members. Focus on the immediate needs of the children and take a one-day-at-a-time approach. Find and use support systems outside of the family. Always maintain a positive image of your children as healers and survivors.

Resources for Parents

Brooks, B. & Siegel, P. (1996). The Scared Child: Helping Kids Overcome Traumatic Events. New York: John Wiley.

Monahon, C. (1997). Children and trauma: A parent's guide to helping children heal. San Francisco: Jossey-Bass.

National Association of School Psychologists: http://www.nasponline.org

National Center for PTSD: http://www.ncptsd.org/facts/specific/fs_children.html

Reprinted from Helping Children at Home and School: Handouts from your School Psychologist (NASP, 1998)

Philip J. Lazarus, PhD, is with Florida International University.

Reprinted with permission from "Helping People Cope with Tragedy & Grief," published by ERIC Counseling and Student Services Clearinghouse.

Counseling Today, Regina Reitmeyer

For many American children, the events of Sept. 11 will forever be intermingled with clips of their favorite early morning cartoons. Crumbling buildings, exploding airplanes and images of people leaping to their deaths from the upper floors of the World Trade Center in New York are still very fresh in their minds.

"Trauma brings a need for predictability, safety, kindness and trust — and all of that has been violated," said Jill Riethmayer in speaking about the terrorist attacks on America and its impact on children.

Riethmayer is director of the Center for Student Assistance at Blinn College in Bryan, Texas, and a member of the American Counseling Association. She trains counselors who work with children and urges them to discuss the event through honest dialogue appropriate to the child's developmental age and to balance that dialogue with a return to normalcy.

"You've got to answer (their) direct questions with knowledge that's in a format they can understand and not give them more than they need, but give them the truth," she recommends. "Then, within that setting, you need to get back to a normal routine as quickly as possible, with them having an open door so you can come and talk more about it."

In cases of trauma, however, "normal" always changes from what it was prior to the traumatic event, so a "new normal" needs to be created.

In her workshop presentations on post-traumatic stress disorder, Riethmayer uses a puzzle that can be rearranged into different shapes to illustrate this re-creation. Reconfiguring pieces from a square into a triangular shape for example, she alludes to the threefold responsibility in counseling for PTSD: Helping to pick up the pieces of what has happened; Trying to arrange the pieces to make some kind of sense and meaning from it; and Empowering the child—or adult —to go on with the "new normal."

Trauma, Riethmayer said, usually produces three effects—isolation, silence and powerlessness. Counselors need to break the isolation by joining PTSD victims in their pain or fear; then, help to them to express their pain or fear in words and finally, empower them to go on with their lives after they have redefined what normal is.

PTSD reaction can range in children and adults from absolutely no response to very emotional responses and will vary according to developmental age, said David Kaplan, ACA president-elect and chair of the Department of Counseling Education and Rehabilitation Programs at Emporia State University in Emporia, Kan. Consequently, 100 different people can be in "100 different places on that spectrum," he said.

Kaplan said very young children—up to six years of age—tend to get concerned about the safety of their parents and their immediate surroundings and try to resolve things they don't understand through nightmares. Preteens and young teens might have the same kinds of issues, but would be a little more egocentric— "How does this affect me? How is this going to change my life?" they may wonder.

Kaplan cites his own experience when President John F. Kennedy was assassinated in 1963. A preteen then, he said his biggest complaint was not being able to watch Saturday morning cartoons that were pre-empted by coverage of the slain president's funeral.

"Sometimes, adults get angry at kids for those kinds of egocentric statements, but they need to understand that that's normal and to be expected," he said.

High school students, too, worry about how the event affects them personally, he added. But—in light of the new war on terrorism and the military strikes in Afghanistan—high school boys also might begin to worry about the draft.

Martha Erickson, director of the Children,

Youth and Family Consortium at the University of Minnesota in Minneapolis, Minn., said adolescents—students in middle school and in their early teen years—might react more strongly to the terrorist attacks than other age groups.

"Part of what happens with adolescents is that they are defining their own identity by virtue of who they like and who they don't like. There's a me/they kind of behavior and attitude that are very characteristic," she said.

One result, she cautions, is a tendency to ostracize or even harass children and other people who are different. "That's something that adults really need to head off, particularly with that adolescent group where those could become really destructive behaviors and just very naturally grow out of what adolescents are doing anyway," she warned.

Like Erickson, Kaplan urges parents to seize this "teachable moment" to ward off the potential for ethnic discrimination. "This gives parents and schools the opportunity to focus on the values of different cultures and give blame for what happened on Sept. 11, specifically to the individuals involved and not to the culture, the country or the religion," he said.

Counselors also express concern about children who have experienced prior loss or trauma. Erickson warns that children for whom PTSD symptoms are reactivated "cannot put that into words and so it may come out as an increase in aggression, a total withdrawal or any number of things, especially for children who have experienced a lot."

While counselors agree that children should be shielded from media coverage of the events, some adults and educators take exception to that recommendation. Susan Tarasevich, crisis management specialist at St. Francis Health System in Pittsburgh and a member of ACA, said television coverage "was a source of division" among educators attending four crisis management workshops presented in late September by SFHS and the Allegheny Intermediate Unit in Pittsburgh.

Some adults argued that it was their "right" to be informed and found constant news accounts helpful; consequently, in some schools, the television was on all day on Sept. 11.

"Informing students in more personal ways may be more productive," Tarasevich advised. "Establishing a safe TV room for staff where broadcasts are aired may meet the needs of adults while returning students to the safety of routine."

One of Kaplan's students unsuccessfully offered similar advice at a school where he was interning. "I think my student was right," he said. "That's a type of trauma for kids to see (the crashes) over and over and over again."

Riethmayer attributes excessive exposure to television coverage to an incident reported to her by a counselor who was trying to help an elementary student identify his goals. As the youngster was manipulating some clay she had given him, he modeled a building and an airplane, and had the plane crash into the building.

"The critical thing to remember is that she had a specific task she was leading him to, but that had no importance to him at all. What mattered to him is what had happened Tuesday morning, (Sept. 11)," she said. "Obviously, he had sat in front of the TV and seen the pictures of what (had really) happened."

Other issues raised by educators attending the workshops dealt with terrorism and possible long-term implications, and ranged from guidelines for parents to adequate planning for safety and crisis response.

Almost immediately after the attacks, SFHS faxed educators in the area a series of guidelines—based on tips from the National Organization for Victim Assistance. In addition to outlining PTSD symptoms, the guidelines urged adults to normalize routines, listen and respond to children on their own terms, provide reassurance and avoid speculation. Additional information from countless sources was available on the Internet.

"Without our even asking, a lot of opportunities for resources came to us," said Ellie Stoehr, director of pupil personnel at Upper St. Clair School District in Pittsburgh. "The amount of time that lagged between when this severe crisis occurred and the time we were able to put something helpful into the hands of parents and our staff was less than 24 hours."

Programs in place throughout the district before the Sept. 11 attacks closely resemble a recommendation by Riethmayer that counselors provide classroom guidance on trauma and its impact, and even on terror and what it means. She suggested that counselors follow up those discussions by encouraging students to ask for additional help if they need it, then form smaller groups with those children to address that need.

With 13 counselors and a school psychologist to serve its 4,000 students, the Upper St. Clair School District regularly provides planned, in-class discussions tied into curriculum units in kindergarten through fourth grade, and additional opportunities for counselors to gather with smaller groups of the youngsters at lunch or in friendship groups.

At the middle school level—grades five through eight—counselors spend half their day teaching a guidance curriculum that exposes each student to a counselor at least once a week. The remaining half-day is spent on more individualized or smaller group support. As result, most discussions of the Sept. 11 events were able to occur during routinely scheduled opportunities at both the elementary and middle school levels, according to Stoehr.

At the high school, where the focus is more on individualized counseling, student reaction turned more toward activism—drives for blood, donations and other items. "The initial response, particularly at the high school level, although this is certainly occurring at other levels, as well, was: 'What can we do? How can we help?'" Stoehr reported.

Because of the country's subsequent response to the terrorist attacks and possible repercussions to that response, counselors remain uncertain as to how long PTSD symptoms might lie dormant. Some estimate six months to a year, while others say it's impossible to determine.

When and if PTSD symptoms surface in some children will likely depend on the way the adults around them are handling their own fear and/or hostility. "Kids," said Erickson, "are taking their cues from adults."

Calls to the Consortium indicated initially, very young children didn't seem to be affected by the Sept. 11 events, but as time went by, they began to express fear. Erickson believes that initially, the attacks didn't look much different than other programs children view on television.

"Young children can't discern between fantasy and reality—and they don't have a sense of geography," she said. "But, as time went on and they saw more of the emotions (their) parents were experiencing, they began to realize through adult behavior that this was something different and this was something more real and more personal."

Erickson also cautions that the talk about chemical warfare and stories about adults buying gas masks can heighten concern among the very young and adolescents. Young children see enough television shows and movies to know that buying gas masks is a scary thing, she said. Older children may have a more sophisticated understanding of the implications of that kind of threat and experience much greater fear as a result.

Other calls to her Consortium focused on parents who travel and the anxiety it causes for small children. "We've had a human face put on this tragedy now

with the stories about the victims and their spouses and families, and that really strikes home for kids," she said.

Her recommendation is that parents be very literal about extra security measures at the airports, provide more details about their trips and call the children once they reach their destinations to reassure them. "Kids find reassurance in details," she added.

Riethmayer said there are two levels of fear. The first level is a global fear: "Is this going to happen to me? How likely is it to hurt or kill somebody here?" The second level is fear for relatives or friends in the military who might die because they are called to defend the United States. Many children—and some parents have never experienced war, so they must face what war means and learn how to deal with it.

Children may confront parents with one other question: "How could God let this happen?" Rather than struggle for an appropriate answer, Kaplan suggests a family visit to a spiritual advisor or even a search on the Internet. "The key is not having to come up with the right answer, but to make it a family activity where everybody discusses it and faces the issue," he said.

Recovering from the shock—for adults, as well as children—is very much a grieving process, according to Riethmayer. It will fluctuate with no particular order from shock to denial to anger to bargaining and finally, acceptance.

Recommended techniques for counseling young PTSD victims range from play therapy for small children to creative arts therapy for teens or even journaling. Riethmayer also recommends bibliotherapy—books and stories that may relate to the child's experiences and provide the child with some new insight or perspective. They can be read to the child or the child can read them independently for a later discussion.

The federal government is also stepping up efforts to assist in identifying effective interventions and improving services for children affected by PTSD. In October, Health and Human Services Secretary Tommy Thompson announced a $10 million child traumatic stress initiative that will be funded by the HHS' Substance Abuse and Mental Health Services Administration.

The initiative provides funds to selected trauma centers throughout the country to help improve treatment and services for child trauma, expand availability and accessibility of effective community services and promote better understanding of clinical and research issues relevant to providing effective intervention for children and adolescents exposed to traumatic events.

Lest counselors forget their own needs in helping

children—and adults—to deal with this national trauma, though, Riethmayer cautions them to do a little self-examination and seek help for themselves, if necessary.

"I think this would be a real good time for scheduled networking," she said. "Counselors in our district meet (every Monday) and let down about what we're dealing with—we do kind of a mini-counseling session with each other. I think there has to be a lot of counselor networking to support each other."

Regina Reitmeyer is a freelance writer in Pittsburgh. This article originally appleared in ACA's *Counseling Today*, November, 2001.

Section Five

Wars, Plane Crashes and More

Counseling Today, Jennifer Simmons

Editor's note: This is part one of a two-part series outlining the unique aspects when counseling Gulf War veterans. Information about helping clients navigate the VA health care system will appear in next month's issue of *Counseling Today*.

With 11 different divisions of counseling just within the American Counseling Association, it's a safe bet that there's a counselor for every concern.

But what if a potential client walked in to your office one day and complained of chronic fatigue, short-term memory loss, problems sleeping and mood swings? But that's not all. What if the client then said they experienced skin rashes, diarrhea, hair loss, joint and muscle pain, unexplainable swelling, extreme nausea and balance disturbances?

And, one last thing—what if they told you they there were a veteran of the Gulf War and had been exposed to anthrax, DEET, depleted uranium and burning oil wells?

It's this combination of symptoms, in various forms, that has labeled the suffering of as many as 80,000 Persian Gulf veterans as having Gulf War Syndrome. However, it's a label that has been summarily dismissed by the United States government as being a valid illness due to exposure to chemicals during the war.

With the government's denial of Gulf War Syndrome's existence as a diagnosable disease, thousands of veterans have turned away from the Department of Veterans' Affairs health care options and are seeking treatment in the private sector, if at all. Even if the government says their illness isn't legitimate, their anger and pain is.

THEORIES AND SEMANTICS

During the Civil War, it was called "army heart." In World War I, it was referred to "shell shock," and in World War II and Korea, it was called "battle fatigue." After Vietnam, the term was "Post Traumatic Stress Disorder."

More than 20 years later, the variety of mental and physical illnesses a solider suffers after a war has been given a new name.

"The Gulf War Syndrome is really very hard to describe or define in a succinct way, but basically it's a kind of psychological and physiological illness that veterans suffer from with a strange assortment of symptoms," said John Eddy, a Licensed Professional Counselor in Texas and an ACA member of 32 years. "It's more defined on the basis of the medical and psychological results of whatever caused this, than the cause."

The first evidence Eddy was able to discover concerning the cause of the illness was in an article in the New York Times in 1997 wherein the Pentagon acknowledged that on March 11, 1991, up to 100, 000 troops were exposed to nerve gas as a result of a demolition in southern Iraq.

"On Feb. 24, 1991, the first day of the ground war, the Pentagon said they detected poisoned gas that day," Eddy said. "We do have concrete evidence that there was some exposure to nerve gas and or poisoned gas. My theory is that this is the major reason for Gulf War Syndrome. This, and some vaccinations, uranium shells and 600 oil wells on fire in Kuwait—or a combination of all of them—are what I believe caused this illness."

Eddy, however, credits the research of Robert Haley, professor of internal medicine and chief of the epidemiology division at the University of Texas, Southwestern Medical Center, in Dallas, as being one of the more influential studies on Gulf War Syndrome.

"(Haley's) research is, I think, the best proof that a so-called Gulf War Syndrome exists," Eddy said. "He says the symptoms of the Gulf War Syndrome are due to damage in deep brain structures caused by chemical damage from combinations of low-level nerve gas, anti-nerve gas tablets, pesticides and DEET-containing insect repellants. His findings would substantiate that chemicals induced this Gulf War Syndrome. My theory goes back to the fact the Pentagon acknowledged the exposure to chemicals in 1991."

Haley believes that because the government is not in agreement over Gulf War Syndrome and its validity, the veterans are "out of luck." According to Haley, skeptics of the syndrome often say that, historically, soldiers returning from wars have had similar problems of combat-related stress. Haley said the government is quick to say that many symptoms of Gulf War Syndrome are also stress related.

"Clearly, after every war in history, there are a number of people who come back and don't do well," Haley said. "This has been used to make a case that, therefore, nothing is wrong with (Gulf War veterans) except combat-related stress. This is a logical fallacy, because nobody ever studied the other incidents with modern techniques because, well, (the techniques) are modern.

"You have to write off those other postwar conditions because nobody knows what they were. What is important is that (the number of people who are seeking medical care after the Gulf War) is way out of proportion with other wars. It's two to three times more than ever received disability after World War I, World War II and Vietnam, and three times as many as after Korea," Haley said. "Those were bloody ground wars and, compared to the others, the Gulf War was a cakewalk. It was five weeks. We controlled the skies and had a four-day ground war. To have two to three times more people seeking service-related medical treatment is preposterous. The Battle of the Bulge was stress. Jungle fighting in Vietnam was stress. The Gulf War was not (as stressful), and for the government to say (Gulf War veterans') problems are stress-related is ridiculous."

The debate between the physiological and psychological sides of Gulf War Syndrome is particularly important for counselors to note.

According to Francis O'Donnell, a Gulf War veteran and the director of Medical Readiness in the Office of Special Assistance to the Undersecretary of Defense (Personnel and Readiness for Gulf War Illnesses, Medical Readiness and Military Deployment), when a group of internists were asked what they thought about treatment for veterans who believed they had Gulf War Syndrome, the majority of the

internists thought the veterans should be referred to a psychiatrist or psychologist. When physiatrists were asked the same question, the majority thought veterans should be referred to internists.

"Medical practitioners are not too sure what to do about this in a definitive way, because both the psychological and physical are involved in this illness," O'Donnell said.

Haley agrees. "Generally, I find that neurologists are the least sympathetic and psychiatrists are the most," Haley said. "This was reported by the VA at a national meeting. The national VA survey, by doctors in the VA system, said that neurologists believe the Gulf War Syndrome is a psychological illness and psychiatrists believe that it's physical in that it's an actual brain injury. But veterans don't want to go to a psychiatrist, because that will confirm to them that they're psychologically ill."

Psychologically or physically ill, O'Donnell does not jump to call what ails the veterans "Gulf War Syndrome."

"I'm hesitant to enter into a discussion of semantics," O'Donnell said. "'Syndrome,' when we use that term, signifies that an illness has achieved certain characteristics by which a doctor can recognize when we see it. With Gulf War veterans, there is no newly unique collection of characters that we've been able to recognize before.

"We're just not there yet. There may be such a thing. There are some scientists who think they have identified Gulf War Syndrome. But we're just not there yet."

O'Donnell said that calling the illnesses the veterans are suffering from "Gulf War Syndrome" is "a handy way to refer to the issue that Gulf War veterans do have medical problems. That's an undeniable truth."

Unfortunately, for the men and women who have the symptoms of Gulf War Syndrome, the "undeniable truth" is that getting appropriate treatment and counseling for their illness, whatever the government chooses to call it, is often the most discouraging part of their journey.

DEALING WITH DENIAL

"A counselor's job will be tough," Haley said. "The problem is that counselors need to realize this is a controversial illness. Even more than that, it's a stigmatized illness."

Haley's disclaimer echoes the sentiments of Russell Porter, a Gulf War veteran and associate professor and chair of the Health and Public Administration for the College of Health and Human Services at Midwestern State University.

"The most important thing is for the counselors themselves to understand the lack of research out there (on Gulf War Syndrome)," Porter said. "Counselors are going to be doing a lot of the ground work themselves to understand both what the cause and the effects are of this illness, as well as the symptomology of it. They will have to create the specific counseling that will apply."

Porter, along with Eddy, presented research on Gulf War Syndrome at the ACA Annual Conference 2001 in San Antonio, Texas, where attendees told them counselors don't really understand the specifics of this syndrome.

To help understand the mindset of a Gulf War veteran who is suffering from what they believe is a service-related illness, Haley said the counselor must understand the situation surrounding Gulf War Syndrome.

"You've got a bunch of (Gulf War veterans) who have brain damage from chemical warfare," Haley said. "The government is denying that these guys are sick. The government tried to convince them that they're just stressed out and they just couldn't take it. Now, keep in mind, these are professional soldiers who were highly motivated to serve their country. This is not a Vietnam situation. These are people who chose to be (in the military) and wanted to do a good job.

"They come back broken people and they're being told that they failed and couldn't take (military service). Besides the physical damages, there is a huge loss of self-esteem. And they're angry at the government for basically reneging on the national contract that we have with our soldiers."

According to Kan Chandras, head of the Department of Counseling at Ft. Valley State University in Ft. Valley, Ga., on Aug. 8, 1994, the House passed HR4386, a $164 million bill authorizing the VA to pay for disability benefits for those who served in the Gulf War. In addition, there is already an existing 1929 congressional act promising health care to those who served in the United States military.

In addition to the frustration with the VA system, there are dozens of stressors on veterans that the average counselor may not know to address.

Austin Camacho, public affairs specialist for the Office of the Special Assistance, said many times, situations that seem "silly" to civilians are actually major stressors to a Gulf War veteran.

"When a person talks about the stress involved with being out of contact with their family, to a civilian it may mean, 'Oh, gee, you couldn't call your wife for two weeks,'" Camacho said. "To a solider it means, 'I might never see (my family) again.' Or you're living in a tent and a guy goes by every morning and he's spraying something in the air. You're busy doing what you need to do so maybe you don't ask what's being sprayed. A few years later you wonder what that stuff was and why they were using it. These could be serious concerns that may be something or may be nothing."

Everyday occurrences -- such as hearing alarms, eating foreign food or drinking water that tastes strange are all potential stressors.

"We hear alarms every day—police sirens, car alarms," Camacho said. "(To a veteran,) when they hear an alarm, it means put a mask on as quickly as possible because you're in danger of being exposed to chemical weapons."

Cultural events can also be major triggers for a veteran. Donald Spalding, a Vietnam veteran who served in active duty in the army for 29 years, has many suggestions based on his 10-year volunteerism as a service officer for the Veteran of Foreign Wars, helping veterans with Post Traumatic Stress Disorder and Gulf War Syndrome.

"I think it's important for counselors to remember that anniversaries and remembrance days are particularly difficult for service members," Spalding said. "D-day, the 25th anniversary of the fall of Saigon—it's days like these that can be very emotional for veterans."

Spalding also suggests being aware that movies like "Saving Private Ryan" and "Pearl Harbor" can affect veterans.

An example of something small having a greater effect comes from Barbara Goodno, director of Public Affairs and Outreach for the Office of Special Assistance.

"For one serviceman, he was experiencing something that triggered an emotional response, and with the support of a counselor who guided him through his memories, they found that the trigger was the opening of a plastic water bottle," Goodno said. "He was one of the first people to arrive in Desert Storm, and one of the big things about that war was the importance of water to keep you alive. You had to drink water all the time. For him it was a series of detective work that he had to do within context with his therapist. As long as the counselor can listen for clues like that, they don't have to have been (in the war) to understand."

Spalding also said there is a need for counselors to recognize the pride felt by many who served in the military.

143

"The service demands a great responsibility, and when returning to civilian life with less responsibilities, it can be demoralizing," Spalding said. "There's a phrase we use for it called 'hero to zero.'"

Because these veterans are dealing with not only the stressors of routine military service, but also with a combination of chemical effects from their time in the service, Chandras believes many institutions aren't prepared for providing therapy for veterans.

"Counselors aren't trained to understand this problem," Chandras said. "It's a different type of problem, and the veterans need to have some people who are trained to understand this disorder."

Again, the issue of anger seems to be at the forefront of veterans' issues, according to Chandras.

"Orienting your life around hate of the government is probably a counterproductive way to live," Chandras said.

And it's not a small number who are potentially living with this anger.

According to Eddy, there are more than 27 million veterans living in the United States, many of them with a dire need for counseling. For Eddy, counseling veterans is, in some cases, akin to saving their lives.

"I've had the opportunity to counsel veterans from as far back as the Spanish American War in 1898," Eddy said. "This is a matter of maybe saving their lives to get them to the right resources. It may help (the veteran), it may help their wives or husbands and it may help their children. It's a matter of life and death."

Jennifer Simmons is Managing Editor of ACA's Counseling Today. *This article originally appeared in the June, 2001 issue.*

Counseling Today, Jennifer Simmons

Editor's note: This is the final part of a two-part series outlining the unique aspects when counseling Gulf War veterans.

Through numerous books and programs, many counselors are more aware of the special needs of Gulf War veterans in therapy, life and understanding. But the question still remains, what can a counselor do beyond the therapist's couch?

John Eddy, a Licensed Professional Counselor in Texas and an American Counseling Association member for 32 years, takes his desire to help a veteran beyond that of the average counselor.

"I contacted Hubert H. Humphrey, who was vice president of the United States at the time, to get a World War II veteran some help," Eddy said. "Sometimes you have to go very high up. I got Humphrey to get the veteran in a veteran's hospital, and then I visited him myself to see that he was getting the proper treatment."

Now, of course, not everyone has the good fortune to have grown up with a future vice president in their hometown, but Eddy's sentiment is what he and other counselors feel should be the lengths one has to go to help their clients.

But first, the counselors themselves must be educated.

"I would think that the first thing counselors need to do is counsel (Gulf War veterans) about how to get through the VA health care system," said Robert Haley, professor of internal medicine and chief of the epidemiology division at the University of Texas Southwestern Medical Center in Dallas. "The VA system is tough, and in order to get satisfaction you have to go after them."

The problem is, many veterans either don't know how to access the services they need or have

become disillusioned with the VA system to the point where they are resistant to try other routes. Therefore, it stands to reason that before a counselor can get a client to a government agency for help, the counselor needs to understand why veterans just may not want to go.

AJ Morris, a Vietnam veteran and a former commander of a Veterans of Foreign Wars and American Legion, has a story. It's a story of a friend who served in the Gulf War and his life hasn't been the same ever since.

"One of my men in the VFW, he incurred some kind of bacteria or chemical that causes his left lower-leg to expand every month, larger than his thigh," Morris said. "(The government) denied having anything to do with it. He goes to the veteran's hospital and they tell him, 'It couldn't possibly have happened in our war.' His own civilian doctors have seen nothing like this. This had to have come from his Gulf War experience. He doesn't know exactly where it came from, but he does know one thing—it's not normal for your leg to swell up in one place.

"After denying him service for several years, they have now sent him to Houston to try to determine what it is, and they don't have a clue in Houston. No one knows what this is. Although they have done testing, no one will take responsibility. This story is being repeated thousands of times across the country for the past year. These hospitals should say, 'You have a problem, let's go take care of it.' But they don't. They deny everything until we can prove it really happened.

"Counselors should be working inside these hospitals to make these guys feel loved and warm. This should be a familial hospital," Morris said. "What we need to have is a policy wherein the veteran's hospitals agree that you are a veteran, and so you have full entitlement to health care from us. It's just a policy situation. It's a bad policy situation."

Bad policy or not, the understanding of the VA

system has become its own stumbling block in the minds of veterans who have had negative relationships with it.

For a better grasp on the rights of veterans, Francis O'Donnell, a Gulf War veteran and the director of Medical Readiness in the Office of Special Assistance to the Undersecretary of Defense (Personnel and Readiness for Gulf War Illnesses, Medical Readiness and Military Deployment), offers his take on the VA's stance on helping veterans.

"My simple-minded take on the subject is that it's basically a law that if you serve in the military and if, during your time in the military, you develop an illness or if you're injured, then the presumption is that illness or injury is service connected," O'Donnell said.

"For a service injury or illness, or the complication thereof, for the rest of your life you are entitled to care by the VA if you are no longer serving," he said. "If it happens to produce degrees of disability, then one might also qualify for disability compensation based upon the degree of disability related to those service-connected problems.'

But, as O'Donnell said, "That's the easy part." "It doesn't matter if that illness is actually caused by military service, but if it begins while in the military, you don't have to argue that cause," he said. "And that's good. It's a real comfort. In the case of disease, it's really convenient. There's no real wrangling about why you have a particular disease.

"The flip side of that issue is that if you just get out of the military and two years go by and you develop a medical problem which you, in your heart, believe was caused by that military service, and if the evidence is skimpy, you may have difficulty proving it was service-related. However, there are exceptions to that. Suppose you worked with asbestos in the Navy, and five years after you got out of the Navy you start noticing a related cancer—you just have to make your case for that. But the burden of proof is on the veteran."

Austin Camacho, public affairs specialist for the Office of the Special Assistance for Gulf War Illnesses, said many veterans misunderstand what the agreement was between the veterans and the government.

"Congress decides what kind of health care the veteran is qualified for and, over time, that system has become very complicated," Camacho said. "It's not an easy thing to know what your veteran services are. Sometimes the people (in veteran's services) don't even understand what they're supposed to be able to do."

Furthermore, Camacho said, veterans sometimes don't know how to ask for services, and some veterans feel they shouldn't need to ask.

"The third aspect is, it's not always obvious how or who to communicate with," Camacho said. "People are comfortable communicating in many ways. If someone wants a voice on the phone, a letter or an e-mail, they can do that (at the Office of Special Assistance). Unfortunately, much of the federal government doesn't offer those options."

According to their brochure, the Office of Special Assistance has a three-part mission—to ensure that all who served in the Gulf War receive appropriate medical care; to do everything possible to investigate and explain Gulf War illnesses, informing veterans and the public of progress and findings; and to put in place all required military doctrine and personnel and medical policies to protect the forces in the future.

The Office of Special Assistance can be a counselor's first stop when trying to get help for a client who is a Gulf War veteran.

Barabra Goodno, director of Public Affairs and Outreach for the Office of Special Assistance, said of her work, "There are (veterans) out there who are tough cases. These people are sick even if you don't understand why they feel badly. If you turn them away, where are they supposed to go next? Our job is not abandoning these folks, but to stay with them. Abandonment is not part of the Hippocratic oath."

Maria Martinucci, team leader of Veterans Data Management in the Office of Special Assistance, described the kind of service a veteran would get if they called.

"There are six of us in our office from 9 a.m. to 9 p.m., Monday through Friday, Eastern Standard Time," Martinucci said. "During that time, we take any incoming calls and talk to the individuals. We're all veterans ourselves, so we're able to deal with the military jargon that comes up. We try to capture what the issue is, even if we can't solve it. We develop a relationship with the veteran."

There are 1,500 locations where veterans can register with the VA Persian Gulf Registry and receive a free physical. If a veteran is in crisis on the phone, they have third-party counselors who can be placed on the phone with the veteran's permission.

Martinucci said, "The biggest thing is that there's someone on the other end of the phone who has been through the same sort of situations (the veteran's) been through. There's a lot of empathy with the person you're talking to."

And this is no small success, according to Camacho.

"Very often, by the time a person has contacted us, they are already carrying a lot of frustration in trying to make a situation work for them," he said. "The biggest problem the veteran is facing is the sense that no one is listening—no one wants to hear what he has to say. Often, the best thing we can do is listen.

"We respond to every e-mail, every phone call and every letter. We see them as individuals. We heard them and we are listening."

Camacho says that often, when they receive an e-mail or letter to the Office of Special Assistance, it indicates the person has already given up and is using them as a last resort. "The first thing they'll write is, 'I know you don't care,' or 'I know no one will help me, but ...' We've have all had this experience of being ignored by a doctor or brushed off by someone in finances while we were in the military. We think of (the VA hospital) as a service organization and they think of (veterans) as a case. Here, we think of the cases as people."

Camacho said he is "embarrassed" to say that he believes the Office of Special Services is unique in the government.

"I would like to think that we represent a lesson learned, and the rest of the government will eventually come around to our way of thinking," he said. "I believe that that personal touch really does make a difference."

And in the face of long-fostered discouragement with the government, a personal touch can be crucial in guiding a veteran to a military health service. And according to Morris, this does not apply to only Gulf War veterans.

"One of the things that we have with these old military guys with a mindset of 'damn the torpedoes, full speed ahead,' is a dedication to the nation," Morris said. "When the doctors refuse to treat them the first time, (the veterans) say, 'Well, this is the result of my volunteering to serve my country, and I don't need to come back to hear you tell me that this is a lie,' and they don't come back."

Morris believes that acknowledging that your country has turned its back on you is a difficult thing for many veterans, both old and young.

"It's hard to tear your country down," he said. "Who wants to attack the system you were willing to die for?"

Morris, himself a veteran, has tried to navigate the VA system on his own and has found that the issue is also spiritual.

"At 60 years old, I never had registered (with the Gulf War Medical Registry), so I finally registered with the veterans hospital," Morris said. "It's been a year since then. It took six months to get my first physical and four months to ever get back to me after I originally filled out my paper work to schedule a physical. I'll tell you if I ran a business like that in America, it wouldn't last six months.

"There's no hospital that could have that kind of administration and survive. The VA hospitals run on such a slow time. If they came up with something that I needed to be treated for, it would be really hard for me to wait six months to a year to be treated."

Officials at the Association for Counselors and Educators in Government did not respond to Counseling Today's request for an interview by presstime; however, O'Donnell reiterated the Office of Special Assistance's commitment to helping Gulf War veterans, especially those who have had a hard time in the VA system, be it due to slow processing or lack of acknowledgement of an illness.

"Our organization wants to help every veteran, one veteran at a time," O'Donnell said.

To contact the Office of Special Assistance, call their direct hotline at 800.497.6261, and to register with the Department of Defense Gulf War Veterans hotline, call 800.796.9699. For more information about Gulf War veterans and Gulf War illnesses, visit www.gulflink.osd.mil or e-mail special-assistant@gwillness.osd.mil. For information on VA benefits, call 800.749.8387.

Jennifer Simmons is Managing Editor of Counseling Today. *This article originally appeared in the July, 2001 issue.*

Counseling Today, Barbara Youngerman Meyer

Approximately two hours after Alaska Airlines Flight 261 nose-dived into the Pacific off the coast of California, Bob Dingman got a phone call from the American Red Cross. So did Nancy Gibelius and Bruce Lockwood.

In addition to being licensed mental health workers, Dingman, Gibelius, and Lockwood are disaster relief specialists, trained by the Red Cross. They pretty much know what to expect when they arrive at the scene—the physical details will be brutal and most of the people to be comforted, including rescue workers, are in various states of shock.

As Gibelius, an upstate New York counselor, who lives in Ballston Lake, explained, "Everyone who comes in contact with the disaster is affected. The violence and destruction generated by a plane crash is horrific. At first, the mind simply cannot accept it."

The call Dingman, Lockwood, and Gibelius answered around dinner time on Jan. 31 summoned them to a hotel at the Los Angeles International Airport. That's where the Red Cross was setting up a support center —a gathering place for family and friends of the 88 people who went down with Flight 261.

"About 240 people who had known or were related to the passengers on that plane showed up," Dingman said.

No grieving person was turned away. The group included children as well as adults, plus many Alaskan Airlines employees, because many of the passengers on Flight 261 had worked for Alaska Air.

The hotel was also the place where news crews came to get a piece of the story. Part of Dingman's job, as a disaster team leader, was to keep them at bay, "away from the people who were grieving. Because the media literally swarms around victims if they can."

While disaster counselors offer a sympathetic ear or a shoulder to cry on—if that's what is needed —they also act as a buffer. "We get between them and anything that could potentially cause them more pain," said Dingman, who nabbed a radio reporter "trying to worm his way into the hotel."

Lockwood, who lives in Sacramento, Calif., said the Alaska Airlines disaster was especially tragic since there were no bodies to bury. Scuba divers couldn't reach most of the remains and those that could be retrieved were difficult to identify. Nor could friends and family visit the crash site because the plane had plunged into the ocean, down into 700 feet of water.

The MD-83 probably crashed when a jackscrew in the tail malfunctioned, NTSB officials said. If the jackscrew becomes warped, the plane can't remain horizontal and takes a nose dive. However, in a report released Feb. 14 by Alaska Airlines, the jackscrew mechanism on the plane was considered to be in good working order prior to takeoff.

"We had a very difficult time helping victims through the grieving process," Dingman, a Virginia Beach counselor, explained. "The enormity of their loss was so overwhelming."

Still, relatives and friends of the passengers on Flight 261 needed closure. The 27-person Red Cross Air Incidence Response (AIR) team, which included Dingman, Lockwood, and Gibelius, came up with a plan.

"On Feb. 3, we brought the victims to Point Mugu. It's a naval base a few miles south of the actual crash site, which was between Point Magu and Port Hueneme," Dingman said. "It was as close as we could get them to their loved ones."

Dingman said he cried as he watched the people, who had been given bottles with corks, scoop up sand and water. "They wanted to take home a memento of sorts. Some of the 200 or so people there walked into the water to say goodbye." Some built sandcastle memorials and topped them with flowers."

Two days later, a formal memorial service took place at Santa Monica's Pepperdine University, chosen because the entire campus overlooks the Pacific ocean. Nearly 1,200 people attended, some traveling in what was probably the biggest funeral caravan to roll through Los Angeles. It included 21 buses and 14 other vehicles.

Lockwood, Dingman, and Gibelius were among the mourners. Their role as disaster counselors, Gibelius said, "was to be a presence, to be there for the victims, at all times." She emphasized that, despite the sadness of the funeral, "we as counselors felt that it was an honor and a privilege to be there."

Approximately 100 mental health workers from Red Cross chapters around Los Angeles worked alongside Lockwood, Dingman, and Gibelius. More counselors were called in from Oregon and Washington state. Overseeing the entire operation was the National Transportation Safety Board (NTSB), which gets its authority from the Aviation Disaster Family Assistance Act.

Mental health counselor Sharon Bryson, who heads up the NTSB's Office of Family Affairs, said Congress passed the law in 1996 following the crash of TWA Flight 800 off the coast of New York. Friends and family of those killed in the TWA crash fought to get an agency established that would help future air disaster victims because they didn't want others going through the confusion they experienced, Bryson said.

"They were pretty much floundering for answers right after that plane went down. They called this agency and kept getting conflicting information. And there was no one to really support them through the turmoil," she said.

Bryson added that the NTSB chose to work with the Red Cross, rather than another disaster response organization, "because it offered a full range of care services. We needed mental health workers, chaplains, medical professionals, and people who would watch children while their parents went through the grief process. We needed people who could provide clothing and, maybe most importantly, we wanted an organization that was experienced."

And experience makes a major difference when dealing with disaster, said Dingman, Lockwood, and Gibelius, who are veterans in this field.

"You get a feel for what to do and what not to do," Lockwood explained. "You come to understand that you are not there to intrude on the people who are grieving. You don't go up to them and ask questions. You simply make yourself available to them, if they want your help."

This isn't the first time Lockwood has assisted the families and friends of airline crash victims. In 1997, when 247 passengers traveling on a Korean plane that went down over Guam were killed, the Red Cross sent him in to help out at the crash site.

"As a counselor my job was to help debrief the rescue workers there," he said. "I listened as Navy personnel, Salvation Army volunteers, medical people, and local police officers talked to me about the horror of what they were encountering during the clean up."

Lockwood said he counseled one young female Naval officer. "She couldn't cope with the gore. She felt it was literally contaminating her, getting on her boots as she walked around the crash site. I needed to help her deal with that so she could continue to do her job."

Lockwood, Dingman, and Gibelius, as well as other Red Cross air disaster counselors, serve as volunteers. Two months of each year, they are on call. "And no more than that," Gibelius explained. "Because the experience of helping out in these disasters is so intense, it's not something most of us could do on a regular basis."

All Red Cross disaster counselors are licensed mental health professionals. They work in teams composed of six counselors, six chaplains, five child care volunteers, and other support personnel. Including team leaders, there are usually approximately 32 people on a team, Dingman said.

Counselors interested in volunteer work should contact their local Red Cross chapter, said Morgan, who has worked seven aviation disasters, starting with the 1982 Pan Am crash in New Orleans. In February she worked side by side with Dingman, Lockwood, and Gibelius.

"Most of the people on these disaster rescue teams know each other," Gibelius said. "There is a camaraderie of sorts and a sense of family because we keep getting called out to worked together."

Gibelius also said she has great faith in the ability and integrity of the Red Cross disaster workers, whether they are paid employees like Morgan, or volunteers. "As I was packing my bags to go out to the L.A. Family Assistance Center, I felt a little nervous. You never know quite what to expect. Dealing with each disaster is slightly different."

On the other hand, she said, "I knew I wasn't going out there alone, that I would always have a shoulder to lean on, too, if I needed it."

Barbara Youngerman Meyer is a freelance writer in Gibsonia, Pa. This article originally appeared in Counseling Today, *March 2000.*

Mental Health Professionals Prone to Workplace Violence

Counseling Today, Peter Guerra

According to a Justice Department Bureau of Justice Statistics (BJS) special report titled "Workplace Violence, 1992-1996" released on July 27, working in the mental health field is one of the most dangerous occupations in the nation. Mental health professionals experience a rate of 80 workplace non-fatal victimizations per 1,000 workers. Only police officers, security guards, taxi drivers, prison guards, and bartenders were ranked higher.

Overall, the report found that about 2 million people a year were victims of workplace violence, with simple assaults accounting for 1.5 million of the total. Simple assault is an attack without a weapon that results in no injury, minor injury, or an undetermined injury requiring less than two days of hospitalization. After simple assaults, aggravated assaults accounted for 396,000 of the total 2 million workplace victimizations.

To many counselors in this country, these are not surprising statistics. Most counselors have known at least one colleague who has had confrontations with clients, and some have their own stories of violence. These confrontations range from shouting to homicide.

One elementary school counselor, who asked not to be identified, said that she referred a child who said she was sexually molested by her stepfather to protective services. The mother of the child found out who the girl told and confronted the counselor in the library at school with four members of the family, essentially trapping the counselor alone. The mother then began yelling and threatening to hurt the counselor, the counselor eventually calmed the mother down. The counselor said it was a scary experience, but it was made worse when her administrator did nothing to prevent future attacks.

Mark Kiselica, an associate professor and co-chair of the department of counseling and personnel services at The College of New Jersey in Ewing, detailed a horrific case of client violence. A colleague of his was working in an outpatient office at Western Psychiatric Unit in Pittsburgh, Penn., was shot and killed by a patient.

Kiselica, who has worked in several inpatient psychiatric facilities in New Jersey, said that he has had a number of close calls. Kiselica said that there are certain clients, such as those who suffer from personality disorders or paranoid delusions, that may lash out at a counselor. However, he said that there are ways to prevent violence and personal harm.

"One of the first things I learned is that there is safety in numbers," said Kiselica. "When I worked in an inpatient psychiatric facility, we encountered out-of-control clients all the time. The hospital had a procedure known as 'Dr. Strong.' When 'Dr. Strong' was announced over the P.A. system, all available men in the hospital rushed to the unit where the alert had been sounded. In this way, a dozen or more men could confront and subdue the patient, minimizing the chance that anyone would get hurt."

Kiselica had this advice for counselors to avoid workplace violence:

1. Never confront a potentially violent client alone —use a team of people to respond.

2. Give the client plenty of physical space—don't crowd the client.

3. Reassure the client that you will not harm them.

4. Encourage the client to think about reasons why the client is capable of controlling him or herself.

5. If the client shows signs of de-escalating his or her anger, let the client walk out of the situation under his or her own power.

6. If the client does not respond to these interventions, the client should be restrained by staff or police who have been trained in the proper procedures for controlling violent individuals.

7. After a client is completely calm, teach the client self-control skills—for example, strategies for recognizing and managing anger arousal.

8. Teach staff the warning signs of a person about to lose control so that early interventions can be enacted before the client is beyond help.

This article originally appeared in *Counseling Today*, September, 1998.

The survey is available in PDF format at www.ojp.usdoj.gov/bjs/pub/pdf/wv96.pdf. Single copies can also be obtained from the BJS fax-on-demand system at 301.519.5550, and selecting document 118, or by calling the BJS Clearinghouse at 800.732.3277. The BJS's web site is www.ojp.usdoj.gov/bjs. See also "Safety issues for counselors who work with violent clients" by Mary Morrissey on p. 6 in the February, 1998 *Counseling Today*.

Section Six

Additional Resources

CDC PUBLIC RESPONSE SERVICE

Fear, Fiction, Facts – Let Us Help You Sort it Out

As a result of the anthrax outbreaks following the September attacks on the World Trade Center, the CDC (Centers for Disease Control and Prevention) established the CDC Public Response Service, operated by the American Social Health Association, in October of 2002.

The CDC Public Response Service provides information, resources, and support to the public about biological, chemical, and nuclear terrorism and other emergency public health issues. Concerns about anthrax, smallpox, botulism, and other biological and chemical agents can be discussed with trained Health Communication Specialists.

Support is also provided to public health professionals, emergency response teams, and those who work in emergency management and preparedness. For free promotional items, please complete the order form on the page following.

The service is accessible in all of the Unites States and its territories seven days a week: Monday – Friday, 8AM – 11PM, ET, and Saturday – Sunday, 10AM – 8PM, ET via toll-free hotlines and E-mail. Services are offered in English, Spanish, and TTY for the Deaf and Hard of Hearing. Information can be found on the CDC's Web site at www.bt.cdc.gov.

English Service: 888.246.2675
Spanish Service: 888.246.2857
TTY Service: 866.874.2646
E-mail Inquiries: cdcresponse@ashastd.org

For More Information, contact:
Edgar G. Villanueva, Health Promotions Coordinator
Phone: 919.361.4851
Email: edgvil@ashastd.org

CDC Public Response Service

Background

CDC Public Response Service is a free public inquiries call center and E-mail service established by the Centers for Disease Control and Prevention and operated by the American Social Health Association as a result of terrorist attacks on September 11 and anthrax dissemination in October 2001. Services are provided for the general public, students, healthcare professionals, public health professionals, and emergency response teams. Clear, concise, up-to-date CDC-approved information and appropriate referrals are provided.

Our Service Goals

• To serve as the point-of-contact between the public's concerns & CDC's response.
• To offer a knowledgeable and informed service to educate the public in dealing appropriately with their concerns about bioterrorism and other public health issues.
• To support coordination among response partners, including medical, emergency management, and public health partners.

Health Communication Specialists are available Monday - Friday, 8am to 11pm, ET, and Saturday and Sunday from 10am to 8pm, ET. The TTY Service operates Monday – Friday, 10am to 10pm, ET. These services are available to the United States, Puerto Rico, and the U.S. Virgin Islands in English, Spanish, and TTY. The phone numbers are as follows:

English: 888-246-2675 • Spanish: 888-246-2857 • TTY: 866-874-2646
E-mail Inquires: cdcresponse@ashastd.org • Web site: www.bt.cdc.gov

---

FREE PUBLICATIONS ORDERING FORM

All materials are free!

CDC PUBLIC RESPONSE SERVICE

Name _____

Name of Organization _____

Address _____

City_____ State_____ Zip _____

Phone ( )_____E-mail: _____

Item	Quantity
Bioterrorism Brochure (English)	(Limit 50)
Bioterrorism Poster (English)	(Limit 10)

Please return forms to: Edgar Villanueva, Heath Promotions Coordinator
P.O. Box 13827 • Research Triangle Park, NC 27709 • Phone: 919-361-4851 • Fax: 919-361-3133
E-mail: edgvil@ashastd.org